A Lancashire Past

A Lancashire Past

A Family Love Story

Kindest regards

J.W. Foulds

J.W. Foulds

authorHOUSE®

AuthorHouse™
1663 Liberty Drive
Bloomington, IN 47403
www.authorhouse.com
Phone: 1-800-839-8640

© 2013 by J.W. Foulds. All rights reserved.

No part of this book may be reproduced, stored in a retrieval system, or transmitted by any means without the written permission of the author.

Published by AuthorHouse   02/28/2013

ISBN: 978-1-4817-8364-4 (sc)
ISBN: 978-1-4817-8365-1 (hc)
ISBN: 978-1-4817-8366-8 (e)

Any people depicted in stock imagery provided by Thinkstock are models, and such images are being used for illustrative purposes only.
Certain stock imagery © Thinkstock.

This book is printed on acid-free paper.

Because of the dynamic nature of the Internet, any web addresses or links contained in this book may have changed since publication and may no longer be valid. The views expressed in this work are solely those of the author and do not necessarily reflect the views of the publisher, and the publisher hereby disclaims any responsibility for them.

Contents

Acknowledgement vii
Prologue ix
Introduction xvii

The Walker Family 1
The Foulds Family 3
Interlude: Away from the Cotton Industry 7
The Hungry 1920s and Sport 10
Radical Changes 12
A Growing Family and a Nomadic Lifestyle 26
A Brief Review of the Walkers 32
A Catastrophe and other 1930s' Musings 35
Moving again 64

About the Author 127
About the Book 129

Acknowledgement

Whatever I and my 3 siblings achieved in our lives was due to the loving family who nurtured us through difficult times.

They were:—   Our Grandfather, James Foulds
Grandmother, Ethel
Father, James Jnr
Aunt Mary Alice, and her husband
James Tomlinson

This book is dedicated in fond and grateful memory

Prologue

Henry Ford is reputed to have said, 'History is bunk.'

I think that Henry should have concentrated on building motor vehicles and not concerned himself with philosophy. I believe, quite firmly, the opposite to Henry. History concerns us all. We are, all of us, living history. I and my disparate family have lived through momentous times, playing our various parts in living history. Most lives are untidy; the lives of members of my family have been no exception. They have been a mixture of struggle, ignorance, misery, blissful happiness, failure and achievement. This is our combined story, although I write almost an entirely personal narrative, with limited contributions from family members. For most of the time about which I write I kept no notes. My principal reference has been an accumulation of family photographs.

The story does not pretend to be impartial, and I make no apology for subjectivity. The importance of the book lies in the recording of an eventful life and the various family members influential in its shaping. I write of my passage through a vanished world, one still rich in my memory. Although many of the relevant places and personalities have disappeared, memories remain. In gathering twilight, the writing a form of therapy, it is an overdue acknowledgement of an immense debt of gratitude. And a dismissal of Henry Ford's blinkered expression.

0 = Colne Town Hall. Built by my Grt Grandfather Thomas Walker.

1 = 4 Walker girls, in finery, with their respective beaux.

2 = Author's Grt Grandparents, James and Mary Alice Foulds

4 = Author's father, James Jnr, as a small, Edwardian, child

5 = Author's Grandmother Ethel, with Father, and his elder sister Florence.

6 = Author's Father, in Chauffeur's gear.

7 = Local Junior football team. Author's Father, captain.

8 = Author, as a baby, with older sister Sylvia.

9 = Author, 2 yrs old. Disapproving of photographer Father.

10 = Father, with toddler author and Sylvia, at Elslack.

11 = The three older Foulds children, Alkincoates Park.

12 = Author's Grandmother Ethel, with her sister Emma.

13 = Author's Father, James Jnr, in politician mode.

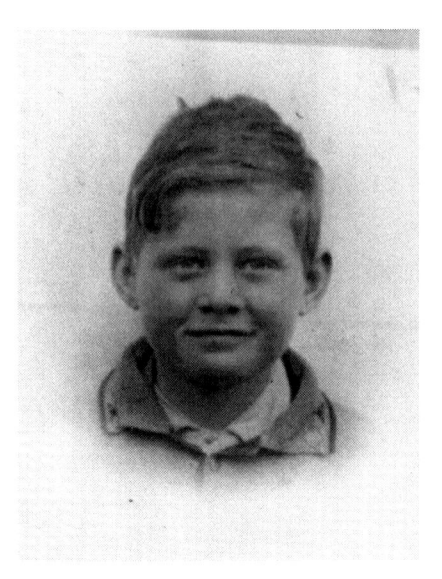

14 = Author, schoolboy aged 7yrs.

15 = Author's Aunt Mary, with husband, James Tomlinson. Honeymoon.

16 = Author's Grt Grandmother, Eliza Walker

17 = Gt Grandmother's 8 children, and surviving spouses, 85th party.

17A = Author, sister and friends, rural pursuits.

18 = Author, aged 10yrs. Silver Jubilee, King George V & Queen Mary

18A = Author's Grandfather, James Snr, aged 70. Defiantly smoking.

19 = The Youth Hostel's clever dog playing dominoes.

Introduction

Colne is situated on the Pennine hills, surrounded by open countryside, the Yorkshire Dales a few miles distant. I was born in Colne in the Borough of Pendle in Lancashire in the year of the British General Strike-1926. A proud Lancastrian, both of my parents are of Yorkshire stock. The predominant families under discussion—the Walkers and the Fouldses—are rooted in the North of England. A mix of typical North Country races, the Walkers are dark-eyed, dark-haired, Celts, and the Foulds are blue-eyed, blond, Anglo-Saxons.

My Great-Grandfather, Thomas Walker, was a stonemason. He deserted his native Yorkshire in about 1880 and joined the workforce, building the burgeoning factories urgently required for the weaving of cotton in the favourably damp Lancashire climate. No doubt with the help of one or two others, Thomas also built the Colne Town Hall, together with the associated Civic Buildings.

Photograph 0 is a picture of this edifice, taken in about 1970, after the stonework had been cleaned of almost a century of accumulated soot and mill-chimney grime. When my Great-Granddad had finished its building, this is how it would have appeared. There is a family story—possibly apocryphal—concerning the twelve-foot square paving slab at the entrance to the Town Hall. It is said that when this slab was laid, a gold sovereign was placed at each corner. Since this story was first told to me by one of Thomas's daughters—my Grandmother—maybe it is true. It is unlikely now that we will ever know.

Additional to the Civic Buildings, the imposing Co-operative Society buildings in Albert Road are further examples of the construction skills of my Great-Grandfather and his Victorian workmates. Sadly, illustrative of 'Cool Britannia' and the consuming greed of the supermarket, the Co-op is no longer the power it was in yesteryear. All the former Colne Co-op emporia have now been variously altered into bistros, unisex hairdressers, and trendy and youth-driven fashion outlets. It is a depressing occurrence, although lately there does seem to be an upsurge from the dormant Co-operative movement. I fervently hope so.

For the present, the Walkers take a back seat while the name of Foulds takes our attention. The name is well established in Colne, and records into the early eighteenth century support this. For our purposes we start with my Great-Grandfather. He was born in Colne in 1831. His name was James; to this day the first son has always been given this name.

The principal employment in Colne from the sixteenth century was, of course, weaving, initially of wool by hand loom. With the arrival of cotton, industrialised production was established. Among the workforce, progressively, so many of the Walker and the Foulds family members.

That then briefly establishes the roots and origins of my family. Now, the Foulds' family patriarch, I believe it is vital that our history is recorded before it is too late. In my passionate belief, it is important, revealing, and quite fascinating—contrary to Henry Ford's dogmatic attribution. Our family has had its full share of notable events and personalities; they must be recorded. It is our contribution to history.

The Walker Family

We have already met stonemason Thomas. His wife, Eliza (née Verity), was also associated with stone. Together with her three brothers, all were involved in the operation of the family quarrying business in Meanwood near Leeds. During their time at Meanwood, one, or perhaps all, of the stonemasons, Verity brothers, as a demonstration of their masonry skills, chiselled from a single boulder a fully functional dog kennel. Perhaps it still exists today; certainly in the 1960s my Dad and a Walker cousin succeeded in finding it. Unfortunately they failed to say where exactly it could be located.

Thomas and Eliza seem to have been a devoted couple. What is certain is that they together produced a large and healthy family of six girls and two boys. However the transfer was organised, the whole family group decamped together to Colne sometime in the 1880s.

The Walker girls were clearly a very attractive lot, as picture 1 shows. Taken in about 1895 it shows the middle four girls in their Sunday finery together with their respective beaux. Facing the camera and on the left of the photo are: Ethel, with James Foulds—my Grandparents; Cissie, with Wilkinson Allison; followed by Hannah, with Fred Lovett; and finally, Emma, with James Hall.

The eldest girl, Mary, with husband Jesse Edmondson, together with the youngest girl, Florrie Whittaker, must have been otherwise engaged at the time of the picture. The two Walker sons, Thomas and Daniel, married twin sisters Nellie and Liza. This pair came to Colne to work initially in service in the cotton masters' houses.

They arrived from their home in Kirriemuir in Scotland, where they had briefly shared a village school education with *Peter Pan* author J.M. Barrie. As was normal for the time, the Walker family were not widely travelled. Once settled in Colne, Cissie and Emma, together with Florrie and their mother, all lived close together in cobble-stoned Oak Street.

Being of close proximity to work in the cotton mills was of significant consideration, and several family members found employment in the Oak Street complex of four weaving sheds.

All of these businesses were powered by a common steam-driven piston engine and its Lancashire boiler, through a system of overhead belt-driven shafting and pulleys.

For their part, sons Daniel and Thomas took a different route, heading back to their home county, Yorkshire. In the nineteenth century and deep into the twentieth, the Yorkshire County Cricket Club authorities refused to include in their sides any player not actually born in the county.

At that time, cricket in England was of great local and national importance; to play for the county was a matter of great pride and kudos. So, duly married, both sons dutifully moved their brides into nearby Yorkshire—in Daniel's case to Earby, while Thomas chose Barnoldswick. While not a major move for either of them—less than five miles—any sons would be 'Yorkies' and would therefore qualify to play for the county cricket team.

To digress slightly, Yorkshire-born journalist and broadcaster Michael Parkinson has recounted the story of how, when his wife was pregnant with their first child, and Michael had been working in 'opposition Lancashire', his cricket-obsessed father had, in due time, kidnapped his daughter-in-law and moved her back into Yorkshire for the birth. Both Michael and his father had in their time been talented cricketers, without either of them rising to the heights of a place in the Yorkshire team. Perhaps a Grandson could fill that aching void. Parkinson Senior clearly thought it worth his intervention.

So that establishes the Walkers. Now to return to the Foulds branch . . .

The Foulds Family

We begin with my Great-Grandparents: James Foulds, born in Colne in 1831 and who died in 1918, and Mary Alice (née Hartley), who was born in Colne in 1840 and who died in 1886. (There is a family story that Mary was Aunt to local hero Wallace Hartley, bandmaster and violinist on board the *Titanic*.)

Photograph 2 shows them in typically stiff Victorian pose. And Great-Grandfather's genes can clearly be identified in my son 170 years later.

They married in Colne in the summer of 1859. Babies soon began to arrive; in fact, from 1861. Sadly, but not unusually for the times, their first three children—all boys—died in early infancy. They were followed successively by Sarah Jane, Born (1868); Mary Ann, B (1869); Benjamin, B (1870); James, B (1875); Alfred, B (1877); and finally, in 1879, by Edith Alice. For the purposes of this story, James will figure the most prominently. He was, of course, my Grandfather, and he was the most significant influence on his descendants.

An interesting statistic: In the year of Great-Grandfather's birth-1831-the population of Colne was 8,806, and the effects of cotton were already clearly evident, when we see that in 1821 the population had been 7,274. (When I was born, a century later, the population was roughly 25,000.)

My Grandfather was one of the ultimate employees in the child labour force in the Victorian cotton industry. With scant regard for legislation concerning the employment of young persons (a euphemism for children), some cotton masters were employing children forty years after enactment of the law. (Factory inspectors were clearly a rare breed.) My Grandfather was working at the age of ten years. Employed as a loom-sweeper, his job was to collect the dust from under the looms that was generated by the weaving process—often while the machinery was still operating. Representing an astonishingly callous disregard for the safety of young people, nay, children, by the cotton masters, it was not at all unusual for those cruel Dickensian times.

Progressively, Granddad was taught to weave by the simple method of 'standing next to Nelly'. In fairly short order he was in control of four looms, for which he was 'rewarded' the weekly sum of £1. The equivalent earnings today would be about £500. On return home he handed his earnings over to his father and was given his 'spending' money—one shilling. Hard times. Today, the equivalent would be about £25. His Monday-Saturday working day commenced at 6 a.m. At 1 p.m. the young persons were then allowed to attend school, for which they paid 6d per week., and today the equivalent would be about £12.

Each morning, the factory gates closed at 6.15 a.m. If the workers were late they were sent home for the day—without pay, of course. This was typical of the working conditions for the 'underclass wage-slaves' at the time. More punitive still, repeated lateness led to dismissal. And after about two years of such slavery, that is what happened to my Granddad. To quote his exact, Lancashire dialect, description of the occasion, 'I geet secked.' He had in fact been late for work twice in one week. He was not unemployed for very long. The Post Office had launched the recent innovation of telegram-delivery by boys on bicycles. My Granddad was the first boy to be so employed in Colne. Sadly he did not reign long.

The Post Office insisted that all their employees had to be inoculated against infectious diseases like typhoid and diphtheria. It was sensible and advanced thinking for the time.

Sadly, James's father did not, or perhaps could not, understand the logic. He refused to allow his son to be subjected to such new-fangled ideas and terminated his employment. For Granddad it was a rapid return to the harsh conditions of the Victorian cotton weaving shed. About this time-1886-my Great-Grandmother died, and soon after my Great-Grandfather re-married.

For whatever reason, my Granddad and his new stepmother, Sarah, seemed to be unable to live together in accord. He was ejected from the family home aged thirteen years. His sister, Sarah Ann, now married, took him in—an arrangement that lasted until his own marriage about ten years later.

Although working a six-day week, Granddad was able, somehow, to follow personal pursuits for pleasure. He enjoyed gymnastics and football, and he played cornet, concertina, and the kettledrum. Most significantly, he was a very accomplished clog-dancer. This talent he maintained into his seventies—, as I can personally attest. See Photograph 18A. (A half-pint of bitter was a dancing catalyst in increasing years, Granddad James always referring to the drink as 'a gill'.) His entertainment skills also extended to Lancashire dialect poetry. He was able to turn these talents to money, appearing in local hostelries when times were hard. (But when indeed were they anything but hard?)

Inevitably, young ladies began to enter into Granddad's life, notably in the shape of one of the Walker girls—Ethel. In the summer of 1897 Ethel Walker and James Foulds, my Grandparents, were married at the Baptist Chapel in Colne. In 1899 their first child, Florence May, was born, her surviving descendants now living mostly in Australia. In 1902 my father James arrived. He was a bonny child, as photograph 4 makes evident. Between early 1904 and the end of 1907, three more sons were born to James and Ethel. Sadly, all died in infancy. To complete their family, Mary Alice was born in 1911. Photograph 5, taken in 1909, shows my Grandma with her two eldest children: Florence May, always known as Florrie, and my Dad, James.

Sometime early in the twentieth century, Granddad moved on from weaving into the more amenable and rewarding skill of 'looming and twisting'. This was a process of preparing looms for the weaving function, carried out in an area remote from the clatter of the weaving shed. My Granddad continued in this job until he retired in his seventies.

Interlude: Away from the Cotton Industry

At the outbreak of World War I there was a radical change for the Foulds family. The army desperately needed to expand all of its base training facilities in order to cater for the anticipated larger armies. The army base at Catterick, North Yorkshire, typically required a rapid build-up of wooden barracks. Afflicted with poor eye sight and responsible for a family, Granddad did not meet army recruiting requirements. Instead—whether called or volunteered—he went off to join the building workforce at Catterick. Although a skilled cotton-worker, he was always keen to expand his knowledge and capabilities. And, astonishingly, my Dad, aged twelve, also accompanied him, and earned 'good money' while developing practical skills with woodworking tools, building wooden barrack blocks.

As hinted earlier, my Grandfather was an unusual man. Both he and my Dad were intellectuals, something quite astonishing for the working class. From my earliest recollection the daily newspaper was *The Manchester Guardian*. Also, neither man wasted time or money on serious consumption of alcohol, characteristically thoughtful, but abnormal for members of the working class. Granddad was an instinctive statistician. In a different time, both he and my Dad would have gone on to university, and both would have been capable of achieving high status in university life. Granddad also strongly believed in women's rights and equality. He didn't agree with the glass ceiling; he was passionate in his belief that girls should be free to do anything that was considered exclusive to boys. His was a very advanced view at the time.

Another of his maxims, expressed in his familiar Lancashire dialect, was, 'Tha eddicates lasses just like lads. When tha eddicates a lass, tha't eddicating a family.' Thankfully, he lived to see, in 1972, the first of his descendants (my daughter) to graduate from university.

Equally, Granddad believed that it was important that boys be taught domestic skills that were traditionally considered 'women's work'. Girls should also be allowed the same domestic opportunities that boys enjoyed. It was a basic policy that would, later, totally influence the lives of me, my siblings, and ultimately, our families. Granddad consistently advocated the philosophy that 'Wimmin shudn't hev ter labour' and to this end labour-saving equipment, as it became available, was bought for use in his households.

The Catterick episode over, Dad and Granddad returned to Colne and cotton. The requirements of the war had meant that there was a heavy and unremitting demand for output from the cotton mills. For the wider family, there was an added problem. Dad's elder sister Florrie had earlier married Fred Senior. Fred was a skilled cabinet-maker, but serving in the World War I trenches, without adequate protection, he had been badly gassed by the Germans. Subsequently, he was never able to consistently follow his trade. Life was an endless family struggle. The workforce included increasing numbers of women and young persons, necessarily making good the erosion of young men into the armed forces. Significant numbers of the Walker and Foulds family girls were involved in that radical change of employment opportunities fo girls.

My Dad was soon employed as a reacher-in—that is, as an assistant to a loomer in preparation work prior to weaving. This function was also a stepping-stone to the more lucrative looming and twisting trade that Granddad performed. Sadly, following the War the industry generally went into decline. Totally inadequate provision had been made for peacetime conditions. Although the carnage of fighting had deprived the workforce of many young men, their absence had been balanced by the tremendous upsurge in women carrying out 'men's work'. But, post-war, there simply was insufficient work to go round. Unemployment rocketed, and the cotton industry was not immune. Although both well respected as skilled tradesmen, my Granddad and Dad were subjected to spells of unemployment. Indeed all of the Walker and Foulds family so employed suffered lay-offs and short-time working.

In 1918 Great Granddad Foulds died in the family house at 2 Elm Street. His accumulated wealth was declared at almost £3,000 (a figure equivalent to about £750,000 in today's money). The earlier estrangement between this hard, unbending man and his son meant that none of this largesse came Granddad's way. The principal beneficiary was Granddad's youngest sister, Edith Alice, then unmarried, and Edith soon became an early car owner in Colne. In a munificent gesture to her unemployed nephew, she gave my Dad a job as her chauffeur. Precisely how he had acquired the necessary driving competence is a mystery. He never did take a driving test, and frankly he was not able to establish in his passengers a feeling of trust even forty years later, to my personal experience. Photograph 6 shows Dad in his chauffeur's rig of the time—a bowler hat and a 'good suit'.

The Hungry 1920s and Sport

For the working class, the 1920s were hard indeed. In the textile trades there was spasmodic employment, low earnings, and precious little hope. For the younger men some relief was available in sport. To mis-quote Marx, sport was an opiate for the masses, a diversion from their, then, bleak existence. Significantly none of the extended family sought release in alcohol; they were modest consumers, at worst. But to a man all were active and capable sportsmen; they were good footballers and accomplished cricketers. In cricket, one was a high achiever—more of him later.

The earlier foray of Great-Uncle Thomas and wife Nellie into Yorkshire had in due time had the preferred result. Great-Aunt Nellie had produced five strapping sons. They all returned to be nearer the family in Colne during the 1920s. Although not of the blood line, Great-Uncle Wilkinson Allison, Great-Aunt Cissie's husband, had also, a generation earlier, been a professional sprinter of significant ability. The house he shared with Cissie was stuffed with prizes he'd won in his pomp. Marble ornaments, an Ormulu clock, cut glass, and a pedal organ, were all additional to the money from prizes and inspired 'insider' betting that supported his family. In due time, Great-Uncle Wilk and Great-Aunt Cissie's family were all keen sportsmen.

The various offspring of the Walker family group played cricket together in the summer in a team known as the Walker Boys. Inevitably it included the names of Whittaker, Edmondson, Lovett, Hall, Woodcock, and Foulds. Indicative of the then importance of cricket, apart from the Colne town team, playing in the Lancashire league, there were many other thriving district competitions. The local churches all played in a Saturday league; mills and workshops had mid-week evening fixtures; and a Tuesday afternoon league catered for tradesmen and shop workers who traditionally worked all day on Saturdays.

In all of these competitions, there was significant participation and no little success from the extended family.

Following their summer activities, all the young men turned to the various local football teams. Most notable in football was my Dad. At his peak, he was a semi-professional for Colne Town in the then Lancashire Combination (10 shillings per match). The equivalent sum today, about £100
Other local teams he played with were Trawden Forest and Colne Skipton Road Methodists, as Captain for both. Photograph 7 shows the latter team in a picture taken behind the chapel wall. Sadly this church was demolished in the 1970s for road provisions. And additionally, at the end of official league seasons, Colne Town FC organised a Mills and Workshops Knock-out Trophy on their 'Old Earth' pitch. Matches were played in the spring evenings, and most of the active family members were involved, including my Dad, into the late 1930s.

Somewhere in the Colne district there must still be the very imposing shield presented to the winners of this fiercely fought annual competition. The accumulated but limited gate receipts from these matches were used to help support and keep alive the Town Football Club.

Decades later, the town football team became better known as Colne Dynamoes FC, who in 1988 played at Wembley Stadium, winning the FA Vase, awarded to junior clubs. When his playing days were over, Dad soon turned his knowledge and experience to coaching junior teams like Colne Grammar School Old Boys and Colne Lads Club.

Radical Changes

In 1923, Dad married Grace Noble of Kelbrook in Yorkshire, taking up residence at 92 Cleveland Street in Colne. Their first child, Sylvia, was born in 1924. In 1926 (the year of the only General Strike in the UK) arrived the author, given the established family name of James with a second name William dedicated to the lost baby brother that my Dad never knew. In 1929, my brother Brian was born, and in 1932 the family was completed with the arrival of Margaret Hazel, for some reason always called Marjorie. Normal for the time, all of us children were delivered at home, by midwife. During a parallel period, Aunt Florrie and Uncle Fred had, similarly, produced four children: Fred junior, Ethel, Donald and Jean. All our family lives, until shortly after the end of World War II, were closely entwined.

All of Aunt Florrie's four children possessed the predominant Foulds' Anglo-Saxon gene: they were blue-eyed, blondes. Of my Dad's four offspring only my brother, Brian, displayed the Walker brown eyes and dark hair. Off these eight first cousins, seven in due time produced blue-eyed, blonde offspring; we could all exchange our children and no-one be the wiser. The power of heredity and genes demonstrated.

Photograph 8 shows my sister, Sylvia, with the author, clearly both blondes, in a theatrical pose in the front room at 92 Cleveland Street, the picture taken by my Dad. Born with an extraordinary memory; my first recollection of life was being in my pram. I would be about one year old. I had been born with six toes on my left foot, one being a 'sprout' off the little toe, lacking any bone, and composed of cartilage and skin only. I was taken to the Keighley Road surgery of our physician, Dr MacAuley, for it to be dealt with. He duly snipped off the appendage and bandaged the foot. From the surgery my mother pushed me in my pram into the Colne main street. I was sat in my pram, outside Woolworths (there was then in Colne a branch of this now defunct chain store), and while my mother was gossiping to a friend, I proceeded to unwrap the bloodied foot.

Photograph 9, taken about that time, shows a, clearly, healthy boy, if one apparently disapproving of his Dad's photography. I am in the backyard of home at 92 Cleveland Street.

The suit I am wearing was knitted by my Grandma, including the fashion-accessory tie. (Throughout her life she was an accomplished knitter and seamstress. The last garment she made for me, when I was aged seventeen, was a coveted cotton gingham checked shirt, woven by another family member.) In those days, it was normal for the doctor's services to be kept to the absolute minimum. Self-medication was the preferred routine. Cephos Powders, Aspirin, Senna Pods, and Sloan's Liniment took care of most ailments.

In the cotton-dust laden atmosphere of the mills, there was, inevitably, penetration of mouth, nose and ears. I can still 'see' my Granddad and Dad routinely flushing out their ears, using a hydrogen peroxide solution injected by eye-dropper! The sight of the bubbles rising, bringing out sludge holding cotton waste, was fascinating. It was clearly an utterly hazardous practice but, to be truthful, both of them retained sound hearing for the rest of their lives. Minor operations like that involving the removal of my surplus toe were, quite routinely, carried out by the family doctor. In my own particular case, Dr MacAuley also removed my tonsils on our scrubbed pine kitchen table. There was no fuss or bother; the patient was rewarded with an ice cream.

Vaccination was similarly a domestic operation. The doctor's costs, then, were paid for weekly. 'The doctor's man' called at the house each week on Friday evening and made collected a shilling or two at each household. This was long before the National Health Service that we now all take for granted.

As well as the doctor's agent, there would also be the milkman, a newspaper delivery person, people collecting insurances, and the coalman visiting weekly. The appropriate monies would be waiting collection: small piles of coins, separately identified. It was not unusual for houses to be briefly unoccupied, but the monies were left to be collected by the individual collectors in un-locked houses. There was no theft of tradesmen's dues; poor we all may have been, but scrupulous honesty was the norm. Even twenty years after my 1947 wedding and departure, I was able to return to my former home and enter the house via unlocked doors. I never possessed a key to that house.

It would be about this—pre-school—time that my naturally enquiring nature led me into an attack of self-mutilation. My mother was an accomplished seamstress, supplementing the parlous family finances with neighbour's sewing and dress-making commissions. All sewing was by hand; sewing machines then were beyond the financial reach of the working class. But one accessory my mother did have was a razor-sharp pair of dress-making scissors.

Possibly impressed at the ease with which material could be sliced, I decided to test the function on my left hand. Maternal dismay, uproar and pandemonium followed at the sight of copious infant gore. I felt no pain as the keen blades cut easily into my flesh, leaving a wound that eventually healed without medical intervention. My hand, however, bears the scar to this day, as testament to the serious nature of my juvenile masochistic curiosity and undoubted proof that male children are a serious health risk demanding constant adult vigilance.

Photograph 10 shows Dad with his first two bairns, by the river side at a local urban beauty spot, Elslack in Cravendale, about 5 miles from Skipton, the capital town of that Dale. It clearly shows the profuse growth of the grasses and flowers typical of the then normal pastureland. The picture also hints at my Dad's enduring passion for the outdoors. Healthy pursuits—rambling and cycling—were duly passed on to all of his children.

Photograph 11 pictures the three elder children in Alkincoates Park, Colne. Sylvia and Jim can be identified by their characteristic blue-eyed, blonde Foulds' genes and Brian can be recognised by his dark-eyed, dark-haired Walker genes. In due time we were all taken on picnics to other local beauty spots, and progressively our horizons widened—from King's Beck, Lumb Spout, and Noyna Rocks to Thursden Valley, Roughlee, and Pendle Hill. Later, cycling was to extend our knowledge of our surrounding attractions and beautiful countryside. Our Dad instilled in us all an enduring passion that in due time we would pass on to succeeding generations.

In our day the picnic season traditionally opened on Good Friday, regardless of weather. I can recall setting out for the Good Friday picnic, to Wycoller, when snow was actually falling!
Quite clearly we were a hardy lot, not easily deterred by weather. However, shortly my life was to undergo radical changes. Picnics or any other such pleasurable pastimes would not be quite so prominent in my young life.

It seems to me that in the 1920s there was not the current established control of education. It appears to me that the mothers decided when their offspring became an unacceptable hindrance to domestic routine; Mother said one day, 'Right, you, school on Monday.'

I could well have simplified the reality, but as a precocious, lively, and enquiring child, I was as abruptly packed off to Park Junior School in Rutland Street aged three years and about six months, early in 1930. By this point I was literate and numerate—blessed with extraordinary genes from my Dad and my Granddad. So it was considered appropriate that I joined the 'baby' class of the school under the care of Miss Townley, even at my tender age. Her classroom was equipped with, among other more educational equipment, a couple of small cots where a tired infant could be put to sleep for a spell. We sat at small, 'paired', polished oak desks, on miniature 'carver'-type oak chairs, with arms, writing with chalk on slates.

Among my classmates, and sharing the double desk with me, was Peter Robinson. Peter unfortunately became the victim of my assault one day, using one of our sturdy little seats to inflict a split scalp on him. Whatever else happened, it didn't seem to adversely affect our friendship or Peter's brain function. A few years later both of us were successful, with five other classmates, in the selective grammar school acceptance examination. Peter's father taught chemistry at Colne Grammar School, later to be one of my respected teachers.

Concentrating now on the subject of cycling, apart from giving my Dad freedom to extend his wanderings in the countryside, it also enabled him to travel further in search of work.

The normal bureaucratic method of seeking employment through the labour exchange could be by-passed. Most towns and villages had their own quota of small cotton mills and these did not necessarily have a regular labour force, particularly in such preparatory trades as that followed by my Dad and my Granddad.

With increased mobility, and thus not restricted to the mills of Colne, Dad, well known and with a skill highly regarded in the district, worked in mills in Nelson, Trawden, Kelbrook, Foulridge, and even into Cowling—five miles distant. By today's standards, he stayed quite definitely local, but in the 1920s and 1930s, recognising the paucity of public transport, a bicycle was a distinct advantage. Short-term employment was the norm, and the ability to, literally, 'Get on one's bike' was a valuable asset. And all to earn, in a fifty-four hour week, the princely sum of between £2 and £3 to feed a growing family. The equivalent today, between £300 and £450.

Impelled by this growing family, and with Granddad's help, Dad turned his hand to food production. At that time it was normal for working men to seek to fill drab, factory-based lives with some outdoor pursuits, and food production was a common activity. Allotments were widely available. In Dad's case, rent was ten shillings per half year per acre. For a brief period, he had two separate gardens, each of one acre. And in today's money, about £75.

Using their constructive skills, developed during the Catterick episode, the pair soon turned open land into food production. A boundary fence, two small greenhouses, potting sheds, and cold frames were all built. And in fairly short order fruit and vegetables were growing. For his part, Granddad turned to poultry. Having first constructed the requisite fences and sheds, day-old chicks were bought. As suggested earlier, my Granddad was a very unusual, extraordinary working man.

He was, in fact, an instinctive statistician. Everything, he turned into numbers; all activities were, wherever possible, treated on a mathematical basis, in what are now considered modern management principles. From the day of arrival the amount of food the chicks were given was recorded. He calculated the week when eggs should be laid; slow birds were given a 'grace' period. When he considered that a bird was uneconomical to feed any longer, it became a table bird.

He gave me my first biology lesson, arising from this matter. A 'lazy bird' had failed to start laying and was being prepared for the table. In the process of 'dressing' the bird, Granddad found that in this particular unfortunate bird's case he had been too quick—by one day. There in the oviduct was a complete, startling, beautiful production line of eggs, commencing with a complete egg, on point of laying, followed by a soft-shelled item and so on, back progressively to a globule of 'frog spawn'. Granddad's expression of surprise and frustration came out as. 'Well, that caps Dolligan!' I was never to know the origin of this expression, but it graphically illustrates his astonishment and disbelief. It also totally characterises my Granddad, particularly his Lancashire dialect.

Of course, at that time all poultry were free range, and generally a cockerel was kept in each pen. And, soon, inevitably, a hen 'went broody' and was allowed to rear the next batch of 'own brand' chicks. Sometimes, to encourage such behaviour, a china egg was left in the nest box. Once a bird ceased to lay regularly it would shortly become Sunday dinner. Household scraps, particularly vegetable waste, were all added to the hen's daily mash. The cleanings from the perches in the hen huts were left to mature for a spell and then used as manure in the garden. Recycling was absolutely our routine. Literally nothing was wasted: slugs, snails, and other garden pests were all tossed into the waiting beaks of the grateful poultry, in their adjacent pen.

With due precautions, it was not unusual for Granddad to allow the hens into the garden to briefly forage for themselves—under strict control. This regulation was particularly so if accompanied by an aggressive and belligerent cockerel, determined to defend his established harem. My younger sister suffered a severe assault from the resident cockerel. Claws, spurs, and beak inflicted a series of leg wounds on Marjorie. It was a forceful reminder not to trust that belligerent bird.

In our childhood, domestic fridges had not of course arrived. The problem of keeping fresh our normal, full cream milk was a summer worry. It was then quite common that milk became curdled. Granddad knew this was not a total loss. The curds were promptly converted into cheese. In summer a muslin bag, dripping whey, was a regular sight over the kitchen slopstone (the bare sandstone equivalent of today's stainless steel sink bowl). The soft curds would be pressed into a bowl and seasoned. Sometimes a few chopped herbs from the garden would be added—long before the commercial products of today appeared on supermarket shelves.

Delicious breakfast porridge was often made from the poultry-food maize meal. Now, such a product has a clever cook's name—polenta. (Forty years on, my brother and his family were staying in our home. Brian and I, late at night, musing on our childhood past, nostalgically recalled the taste of maize porridge. Next morning, early, a visit to a local wholefoods shop produced the necessary maize meal. And for our next breakfast, a delighted Brian and I [the cook] were young again, remembering mealie porridge of long ago childhood days.)

Granddad's productive skills extended further than food. In the garden a small bonfire was always burning, particularly for the destruction of pernicious weeds. As a by-product, potash-rich wood ash was produced as fertiliser. Additionally, this was used to produce washing soap, in bars. Fat that was rendered down from butcher's off-cuts mixed with wood ash produced a very effective soap.

It was not quite smooth, toilet soap quality, but at that time it did prove to be perfectly useable washing soap.—an early demonstration of sound use of natural resources, long before the current 'Green Revolution'. Wood ash, chicken manure, tradesmen's horse droppings and leaf-mould rapidly developed the land into fertile production, almost year-round.

On one notable occasion, the circus came to Colne. Apart from clowns and acrobats, the big top entertainment of the period traditionally included a wide variety of animals. This particular circus featured a troop of elephants. The circus was situated in Skipton Road, in what then was Bowker's Farm. The elephants were all tethered in the open. In very little time, the pile of elephant waste was enormous. The potential free-issue fertiliser was a magnet for my Dad.

I was instructed to take the wheelbarrow and collect masses of the stuff. I don't remember how many trips I made, but I do recall Brian producing a splendid tomato crop from the manure that I collected. I sometimes dreamily wonder how many can boast such a bizarre fertiliser and have eaten the resultant, tasty vegetables? It was so characteristically resourceful of my Dad to recognise the potential of elephant dung.

The routine use of the products offered by nature without dependence on the use of chemicals was absolutely typical of the time. Although there was some emerging evidence of chemical pesticides, they played no part in our garden. For example, any attempt by the cabbage white butterfly to leave eggs on the leaves of our brassica crops was forestalled by juvenile fingers. Any escaping and making it to the caterpillar stage only meant a treat for the hens. There was some use of insecticide spray, but the liquid employed was definitely organic. Both Dad and Granddad smoked a pipe. Then, almost without exception, adults smoked tobacco. The accumulated dottle from pipes and the ends of cigarettes were saved. Soaked in water a spray solution from the nicotine dealt adequately with most garden pests. An alternative was also produced from a solution of soft soap and water—ecologically preferable, and a great deal less costly than chemicals.

Behind the greenhouses were large, wooden tubs. Principally, they collected rain water off the sheds and greenhouses. However, three were employed in the production of different liquid fertilisers. The first had, suspended in the water, a Hessian sack of stable manure; the second had a sack of chimney soot; and finally the third contained the watered contents of bedroom chamber pots. Unfortunately, there was no piped water supply to the garden. In summer dry spells the collection of rain water was miniscule, at a time when the water needed to develop produce was at its highest. It became a normal requirement that a garden visit routinely meant that a container of water was taken, however small. It was for us children, a penance. As I said earlier, nothing was wasted! And the resultant produce was a significant contribution to the table.

All the normal vegetables of the day were grown—potatoes, carrots, turnips, swedes, parsnips, leeks, peas, and beans of broad, French, and runner varieties. All the normal brassica varieties—cabbage, cauliflower, and sprouts—were also grown. However, indicative of Dad's advanced thought, crops included very unusual varieties like kohlrabi, celeriac, sprouting broccoli, and kale.

The juicy stem of a raw kale plant, peeled and sliced, was a real childhood treat. Among the various onion family members, a multiplying, year-round item of-spring onion type was grown, similar in development to chives. When I later married, a root of this productive plant accompanied me. Its successive offspring lasted twenty years. From the two small greenhouses, tomatoes, cucumbers, and marrows were all taken.

Outdoors, all manner of soft fruits were available for us—raspberries, blackcurrants, gooseberries, and strawberries. Unusual domestic fruits like loganberries and blackberries trained up a pergola of sturdy tree branches, another of Dad's constructions.(I particularly and ruefully recall a blackberry variety called 'Himalayan Giant', a savage, spiky and vigorous plant. Its vicious long thorns protected the juicy fruits from thieving juvenile fingers, and I think my Dad knew what he was doing when he planted it. It was almost a triffid; certainly it drank a drop or two of my blood!)

For several years, my elder sister and I, press-ganged into the garden workforce, had the boring task of 'pricking-out' box after box after box of seedlings in the sheds, often by candlelight.

The seedlings were then grown on in cold frames, some for sale door to door and others, as appropriate, for planting in flower, vegetable, or greenhouse beds. Mature flowers could also be hawked locally, generating welcome cash. Of course, both of us were paid on a sales output basis—one penny per shilling of sales. And equivalent to twelve and a half percent.on sales. Exploitation of child labour! We neither knew nor disapproved of this early exposure to the connection between labour and reward. However, when brother Brian was press-ganged into the sales-force there was definite *rebellion*!

Brian proved a very reluctant salesman. He was adamantly, resolutely, and defiantly opposed to confronting the public. He much preferred to work in the greenhouses, becoming a thoroughly competent gardener. It was a skill he retained for the rest of his life, an enduring credit to his Dad's tuition.

Food and products from unusual sources

If we were to believe modern comment, the impression could be created that food from nature is a recent discovery. For our family nothing could be further from the truth. We knew about salad stuffs freely available for the picking. In my childhood, sorrel, chickweed, feverfew, young lime tree leaves, and watercress were often included in salads. In the garden any dandelion that had escaped being uprooted would have a plant pot 'hat', in due course blanching into substitute chicory. In due season, mushrooms, blackberries, bilberries, and crab apples, could all be gathered from the outdoors.

Coincidental with the gathering of the produce, before domestic refrigeration, provision had to be made for as much as possible to be variously preserved. Using salt, spices, vinegar and so forth, pickles and chutneys were packed away for later. It was a joint—family—operation with longer-term benefits as we all became parents.

A cast brass jam pan was purchased by Granddad. It was an annual event for surplus fruit to become jams or jellies. Later, this pan became a treasured piece of family kitchen equipment, passing through successive generations. Now, eighty years later, my son and his industrious wife have it, and to my great satisfaction, my only Granddaughter is keenly being introduced to its use.

Although probably from questionable origins, game was not at all an unusual food in my childhood. My Dad and many of his cousins ranged far and wide in the surrounding countryside, despite the rigorous and watchful eye of gamekeepers. Landowners, although reluctant to see strangers on their property, failed to prevent the 'lads' from keeping rabbits under control and part of our protein intake. Nowadays, despite the ravages of myxomatosis, rabbits have recovered and are badly out of control in the countryside while the urban population has forgotten how once they were part of our normal diet.

The usual method of catching rabbits did not involve noisy firearms. Ferrets and nets were, generally, all that was required. Dad, however, separately, employed an extraordinary technique.
He was a very speedy runner. He would hide himself from the vision of grazing conies, suddenly leap up and sprint towards his prey, making as much noise as possible.

Momentarily the rabbits panicked, lost their bearings, and forgot exactly the direction to the safety of their burrow. Dad's objective was to get between the prey and its burrow. If he was successful, the rabbit would run for the nearest haven, which in our locality was usually a dry stone wall, with plenty of spaces, but crucially lacking escape exits. Dad then simply pulled the rabbit from its bolt-hole and applied the *coup de grâce*.

At that time all the local streams had healthy resident trout populations. Dad and his like-minded cousins knew how to harvest this tasty food-source without any tell-tale fishing tackle. Before the advent of sheets of plaster-board, the interior walls of all new houses were finished by a hand-applied coating of wet plaster, laid on by hand-trowel. This plaster was freshly mixed from quick-lime to which requisite amounts of water was added. The same lime was also used by farmers as an addition to stable manure to sweeten and enrich their fields. There was, therefore, the ready availability of quicklime for other, nefarious, use. A party of 'poachers' chose a pool where they had located a good head of fish. The party was halved, and one team was stationed at the pool entry and the other at the pool exit. At an agreed signal, those at the pool entry would throw into the stream a few handfuls of quicklime. When mixed with water, quicklime boils vigorously and simultaneously takes up the oxygen from the water. The fish population comes to the surface, temporarily stunned and gasping for oxygen. The 'collecting' party at the tail of the pool swiftly gathered up sizeable fish, leaving the remainder to float past. They are not poisoned, just briefly deprived of oxygen, and they quickly resume normal behaviour. Generally, a single pool produced sufficient fish—and, of course, speed was the key for a possible rapid retreat.

Although never an eyewitness to such an operation, I did just once see the outcome, with the subsequent distribution of the night's catch. I would have been about two years old. Put to bed on a hot night, and sleepless, I could hear downstairs my Dad's voice together with several of his cousins, always referred to as my Uncles. Curiosity finally impelled me, very quietly, to walk down the staircase. And what a sight before my eyes! There on the kitchen table was a three-gallon white, enamelled bucket, full to the brim with glistening trout. It seemed a very welcome addition to the week's food!

Now many of such once sparkling streams are sterile and chemically choked drains, almost entirely devoid of life, consequent of the increased use of chemical fertilisers as farmers are pressured to reduce costs and produce more and more from the same area. Once, the farmers nourished their land with natural products, and we had clean streams with resident wildlife. One final source of food, which in these days of increasing concern for wild birds is almost shameful, but related to the circumstances at the time is defensible, was the collection of wild birds' eggs for human consumption.

Ground-nesting birds like peewits were the major targets. At that time there were scores of breeding pairs on every farm. In spring their wheeling aerobatics were a joy. Now much less in evidence, I'm ashamed to remember the countless numbers of wild birds' eggs that I ate. Then they were simply a source of food. At that time, and even decades later, it was also possible to purchase peewits' eggs from 'quality' emporia like Harrods or Fortnum & Mason. What's sauce for the goose was in our eyes surely sauce for the gander. Sadly, the peewit had no input.

And, as an afterthought, the nearby River Ribble had at that time a teeming population of native crayfish. I cannot honestly include them as a personally important contribution to diet.

Dad took me on a—cross-bar-mounted child's seat on his cycle to the river at Paythorne. There in the depths of the crystal clear water were a number of these strange crawling things, possessing threatening, waving nippers. I do recall that Dad soon had a parcel of them in his cycle cape, and it was a quick ride home to deal with them.

As I also recall that I was not greatly impressed. It was a fiddly meal, too much fuss, and inadequate reward. (Thirty years later while working in Sweden I was invited to join a jolly, rural-based, summer festival, communally consuming huge piles of crayfish, made even more difficult by the addition of melted butter. It was still not a really satisfying meal as I recall.

The event was much more memorable for the repetitive toasts in neat Swedish Schnapps. At the evening's end, it was rendered unforgettable by the sudden, alcoholic, decision of my English colleague to somehow reach a stand, lurch past and dive, fully clothed, into the adjacent lake. It was not the effect of crayfish!)

One other unusual source of food was possibly as a result of an initiative by Dad and Granddad. At the time there was a weekly livestock auction in Colne. When in employment, they would arrange for a friend to buy a bull calf for a few shillings. To the farmer, heifer calves were the ultimate source of milk-production and therefore of value. Only a single bull was required in the locality. For this reason bull calves were of little value and were sold as quickly as possible. The animal bought by the family would be discretely grazed and fattened, usually on the football field.

We—the children—were unaware of such arrangements, but the animal would, oddly, without any prior indication, suddenly disappear. Dad had a pal with a small butchery business. Public health was clearly less vigilant back then. Sometimes a calf was not available, and a pair of billy goat kids costing very little would appear and in due time vanish. Resourceful, my Dad!

The truth was that we were poor. We were living through hard times; everybody in the locality was poor. Our adults all shielded us from harsh reality. There was no television to tell us how much better off someone else was; there was no 'celebrity' to parade before us the latest 'must-have'. We were blissfully ignorant and happy despite depressed circumstances. Few children went hungry for long, certainly in our sphere. Elsewhere, there was no doubt suffering, of which we remained ignorant. For the adults, the reality must have been painful, but we children were shielded.

A Growing Family and a Nomadic Lifestyle

92 Cleveland Street lies in the middle of a typical terrace of stone-built Victorian houses on the eastern edge of Colne. Facing the front door across a then unadopted road was a conglomeration of hen—or pigeon-pens and fenced garden plots.

Adjoining them was 'Old Earth', the home pitch of Colne Town FC. It was a notoriously sloping pitch which, it was claimed, gave the uninformed opposition a severe handicap. The ground was situated on the land of the farm with the same title. Facing the back of Cleveland Street then was a dusty and rutted space on which the local children played out their own sporting fantasy FA Cup Finals or, in the summer, cricket Test matches.

Because of the almost total absence of motor vehicles, we were quite safe playing games in the street. In the immediate locality of 400 to 500 houses, there was, literally, a single privately owned car. That belonged to the Barritt family. Mr Barritt was the manager of one of the larger cotton mills.

At the end of our terrace were more hen pens and some gardens and allotments, including one which Dad briefly tilled. A periphery footpath meandered on to meet the nearby Byron Road, the main East Lancashire thoroughfare to Keighley and West Yorkshire. Only from the east was Colne approached by the urban, East Lancashire corridor, through neighbouring Nelson, Burnley and so on. Otherwise, the town was surrounded with open countryside. To the south and east were Boulsworth Hill and the moors bordering Brontë Country. And only a very few miles distant to the north were the Yorkshire Dales.

Less than a half mile from Cleveland Street was open country with birds like snipe, peewits, and curlew. A couple of miles further on was the Kelbrook Moor. Sporting and shooting rights were owned by local industrialist Teddy Carr, his land patrolled by vigilant gamekeepers, watching over grouse and golden plover. (Later, this area, in spite of the continuing presence of the gamekeepers a recurring challenge to adventurous lads, intent on pursuing their own interests.)

Despite the family finance limitations, Colne and district was ideal for raising children. There was almost unrestricted freedom to roam and, then, parental vigilance was at a much lower necessity than, sadly, now is the norm. All of the nearby Cleveland Street allotments and pens, with the adjacent open space, were, post-World War II, converted into a Council housing estate. The 'Old Earth' football ground with its associated farm together with the adjacent Lob Common Farm became the site of the secondary education Park School.

In my Dad's, and my, childhood the school of this name was an integral part of the infant, junior, and senior schools complex in Rutland Street. The two junior educational establishments still operate in these Victorian buildings. The stone-built houses in Cleveland Street, typical of the provision for the cotton workers, were 'two up and two down'. In other words, there were two bedrooms, a 'front room' and a living kitchen.

In the flagged backyard was an outside lavatory flushed by an ingenious tippler system, which progressively collected waste kitchen water through drains into an underground, pivoted tank that, when filled, became unstable, over-balanced, and tipped its accumulated contents down the long drop waste tube leading to the main sewer. It was an early water-flushed toilet system that, sadly, could have tragic consequences for inquisitive children.

Adjacent to the toilet, with its scrubbed white pine seat, was the coal shed. All houses then had open coal fires, burning shiny black nuggets costing about 10p per hundredweight. And today, the rquivalent cost would be between £15-£20. They produced, of course, voluminous, smoky atmospheric conditions, sometimes creating the notorious pea-soup fogs only solved by clean air acts thirty years later. But the sooty chimneys, necessarily swept frequently, made a horticultural contribution, so the universal use of coal wasn't entirely negative.

The 'bathroom' was suspended, in the yard, from a wall-mounted hook; in other words, it was just a zinc-coated hip bath. A weekly bath was the norm, with the bath in front of the open, kitchen fireplace, filled with hot water from either the fire-back boiler or scooped from a heated tank built into the side of the fire-range. This was a tedious and time-consuming operation in terms of both labour and coal. The result was that bath night was a family affair, with the single filling of the bath used for the entire family. Modesty was preserved by the organised use of other rooms and transfer to bed after drying.

During my early childhood, lighting was provided by coal-gas from the town's own gasworks, burning on a single gauze mantle suspended from the ceiling. The illumination thus provided was the equivalent to that provided by about a twenty-watt incandescent electric light bulb. A local wag described the light generated as the equal of two glow-worms in a bottle! For reading, writing, or domestic functions like knitting, sewing, or repairing clothing, additional illumination was provided by paraffin lamp or candle. And for bedtime, a candle mounted on a saucer was not unusual.

And of course the only space heating came from the open fires. Sitting near to the blaze was on a seniority basis. The open chimney and the fire itself meant a continuing inflow of air, or more accurately, draughts, through rooms. Those furthest from the fire had a back cooled by incoming air. Centrally heated homes were a luxury of the distant future.

Cooking could be by a selection of the open fire, an oven, like the hot water tank, built into the side of the coal-fired range, or, unusually, by a gas-oven, with on top, radiant ring-burners.
The rent for such housing was minimal—five, six, or seven shillings from a wage of between £2 and £3 pounds per week. A nomadic lifestyle was not at all unusual. For a reduction of one shilling in weekly rent, or perhaps a better standard of decoration, families would easily move house. Today's equivalent of 1 shilling, about £10

With minimum possessions, a handcart, the freely given help of a few brawny relatives, or at best the hire of the farm—or the coal-cart, moving house was of little consequence. As an illustration, from birth, to my marriage twenty-one years later, I lived in a total of ten different terraced homes, simultaneously racking up attendance at five primary/junior schools and one grammar school by the age of sixteen.

Photograph 11 shows the three elder children arranged by our amateur photographer, Dad. Sylvia is trying to read a story to her disinterested brothers, in the surroundings of the then bandstand of the municipal in Alkincoats Park. The two elder children clearly display the predominant Foulds' blue-eyed, blonde-haired gene while Brian has the dark-eyed, dark-haired complexion of the Walkers.

For the next three to four years, we lived in six different houses, ranging from School Lane in Kelbrook via four separate Colne addresses to Nelson. One of the Colne houses, at the top of Heifer Lane, my Dad set about buying for £200. He was possibly helped by Granddad who already owned the house he, Grandma, and Aunt Mary shared in terraced Fern Street. As I have already noted, Granddad was a very unusual man; for a working man to own his house seventy-five years ago is incredible. The same house would now cost about £125,000!

Cleveland Street runs parallel to Oak Street, where, of course, lived three Great-Aunts and Great-Grandma Walker. A hungry lad could call at any one of them on the way home from school and wheedle a jam butty, half a sadcake (the local equivalent of Eccles cake) or perhaps the standard, working-class Lancashire stand-by—a sugar-butty, to stave off malnutrition before staggering on the final 400 yards to home. Somehow, despite straitened times, our wider family was always generous with all of the family offspring.

At that time, the primary school curriculum featured community singing in the school assembly hall on Friday afternoons. Those wonderfully committed teachers remain bright in my memory still—almost eighty years later. Each and every one of Miss Townley, Miss Tierney, Mrs Fisher, and Miss Brown taught us a love of singing. Their own enthusiasm, indirectly, introduced us to folk, traditional, and nationalistic songs like *Men of Harlech*, *Down Yonder Green Valley*, *On Richmond Hill*, *Bobby Shaftoe*, *Who'll Buy My Caller Herring?*, *Bonny Blue Bonnets of Dundee*, and many, many others.

Their enthusiasm came flooding back to me the very first time, thirty years later, when I arrived in Carlisle, where those 'blue bonnets came over the border'. Their passion for singing returns again and again, whenever I hear one of the provincial, folk, and country songs I was taught in the assembly hall of Park Junior School. Clearly, I must have been enthused then, because every Friday afternoon, after singing, I went to my Great-Grandma's home, at 58 Oak Street, and sang for her all of that afternoon's programme. There was, conceivably, an ulterior motive. After the recital, Grandma would delve into the depths of her apron pocket and produce the reward—a barley sugar twist.

The dedicated teachers responsible for my early education were notable, of course, for more than just generating in us children a love of singing. Teaching, often by the rote or repetition systems now largely discredited by modern leaders in education, turned out pupils with apparently higher standards in numeracy and literacy than appears to be the current norm. Simple arithmetic teaching included mental sums to a standard astonishing to today's adolescents. In supermarkets, young checkout operators are quite unable to comprehend my simple mental arithmetic competence taught to me at Park Junior School seventy-five years ago. We were taught poetry that I can spout to this day. History was not neglected, either. In the 'top' class, Miss Tierney was responsible for me bursting into tears in about 1980 when first standing before the Bayeux Tapestry. As soon as I saw this historic embroidery I was transported back to Miss Tierney's Park School class, listening transfixed to her explanation of events in 1066, using as illustration the panorama of the Battle of Hastings/Bayeux Tapestry, folded into our maroon-backed history textbooks. And there I was, standing before the genuine article. But, in reality, I was ten years old, listening to Miss Tierney, and the emotion was, briefly, overwhelming. It is eloquent testimony to the quality of primary school teaching that we enjoyed and the extended effect it had on me.

A Brief Review of the Walkers

As was noted earlier, Great-Uncles Daniel and Thomas decamped into Yorkshire with their sister-brides. Daniel never returned to Lancashire, living for the rest of his life in Earby. In his case the possible expectation of providing County cricketers for Yorkshire failed. Great-Aunt Liza delivered only a single child, a girl—Jean. Like the majority of the family, Daniel worked in the cotton industry. In a different era he would undoubtedly have become a talented engineer. He had an instinctive flair for design, and improvement of the ancient Lancashire-style weaving machinery and equipment. Later, he was able to provide a good living for his family as a self-employed 'engineer'. Whether any of his ideas were patented is not clear now. But what is certain is that one of them (concerning pirn-winding, a preparatory function of weaving now obsolete) was taken up by a local manufacturer and was a profitable idea. It became the basis for a thriving, lucrative, but short-lived, business.

Daniel and Liza decided that their sole child should be provided with significant advantages relative to the working-class norms. Jean was clearly a bright child, and she was educated privately. In about 1930 she was the first Earby girl to take up university education, at Edinburgh, graduating with a first-class honours English degree. Characteristically, Daniel ended his working life as a semi-skilled engineer at the nearby Rolls-Royce factory during World War II.

Brother Thomas with wife Nellie had successfully raised five healthy lads in Barnoldswick before returning to Colne. Donald, Jimmy, Thomas, Hughie, and Kenneth were all in their time talented local sportsmen. The jewel in the family sporting crown was the youngest, my 'Uncle', K.J. (Kenneth) Walker. Barnoldswick CC is a member of the Ribblesdale League, and as a youth Kenneth began his organised cricket career in the town of his birth. His talent steadily lifted him, until early in the 1930s he was opening the town batting. Not only that, but for three successive seasons during the period he was top of the League batting averages. Inevitably, his ability was brought to the notice of the Yorkshire CC authorities. He was invited to the winter nets at Headingley. Kenneth was under serious consideration for a place on the County ground staff, a first step on the ladder to a place in the County XI.

At that time, the Yorkshire CC side was very powerful. Competition for places at Headingley was fierce indeed. Kenneth was opposed by a player from Pudsey St Lawrence, in the Bradford League. His name was Leonard Hutton. For him the future became very bright indeed, with him ultimately scoring the then world record batting total of 364 for England against Australia at Lords in 1938. Finally he became of captain of his country, with the associated adulation and riches. For Kenneth, it was lost opportunity, a return to bricklaying, soon after the army, where he was grievously wounded in the North African desert campaign and an early grave.

Kenneth's eldest brother Donald's life was almost as dramatic. He worked in cotton. As war loomed in the 1930s the government realised that engineering productive capacity would have to be radically expanded. A government system of accelerated training courses in engineering skills was set up. Workers like weavers, accustomed to the operation of machinery, were ideal trainees. Suitable trainees were identified as 'semi-skilled' and allocated to appropriate functions in the engineering workforce. Donald was one so trained. As a semi-skilled machinist he was directed into war production in Coventry. He was there in an air-raid shelter when the German Luftwaffe blitzed the city on the night of 14/15 November 1940.

In the morning he emerged from his shelter into the shattered city bewildered and traumatised but thankfully uninjured. He set off walking away from the devastation, and he kept on walking until he eventually reached Colne.

He never returned to Coventry. For the remainder of his life he could not forget his time under the bombs. There was then very sketchy medical understanding of what is now known as post-traumatic stress disorder. Reportedly the rest of Donald's life was so adversely influenced.

A Catastrophe and other 1930s' Musings

Despite the depression in the cotton industry, with limited work and low earnings, the extended Walker/Foulds' clan generally stayed local. However, other opportunities further afield began to attract the interest of some of the younger family members.

My Dad's cousins, James Hall (the youngest son of Great-Aunt Emma) and Wilfred Woodcock (Grandson of Great-Aunt Cissie) jointly sought to escape Lancashire's limitations. James had been spasmodically working in the mills. Wilfred was a farm labourer earning the pitiful wages at the time in that industry. Then in their late teens, attracted by the reportedly high earnings in the emerging car industry, the pair decided to leave Lancashire for the Midlands. Sadly it was a decision with tragic consequences. After work the two enjoyed their leisure together, including on the waters of the River Cherwell, the infant River Thames. On one such an outing, in a Thames rowing skiff, James and Wilfred got into difficulties. The immediate outcome was that they both fell into the river.

Wilfred was a strong swimmer while James could hardly swim at all. Whatever the particular sequence of events, calamity followed. Wilfred drowned while, somehow, James survived, to return, alone, to a devastated Oak Street. Wilfred's family lived at No. 39, James's at No. 55, and the grieving Great-Grandma Walker resided at No. 58. Whether or not James was permanently affected by the catastrophe, the truth is that apart from war service in the RAF, thereafter he lived the remainder of his life in Oak Street. On marriage he moved from No. 55 to No. 57, his home until his death.

James's mother, Emma, and my Grandma, Ethel, were devoted sisters and inseparable friends. Photograph 12, taken about that time, should make clear why they were so frequently referred to as twins. In the middle of the twentieth century there were two cinemas in Colne: the Savoy in Market Street and, in Newmarket Street, the Hippodrome. Each had a mid-week change of programme. Irrespective of the films on offer, and as family finances allowed, throughout autumn and winter Emma and Ethel determinedly attended the cinemas four times each week. Both were dedicated cigarette smokers.

For my Grandma, a night at the cinema was not entirely to do with personal pleasure. She was a very skilled operator with knitting needles or a crochet hook. Sitting in a darkened cinema and lacking any pattern, avidly smoking, it was not at all unusual for her to complete a baby's 'donning' for the latest family infant. Nowadays, smoking in public places, strictly outlawed. She managed this for her Great-Granddaughter Jennifer—my own daughter, born in 1950. Now, such hand-crafted, lovingly and practically produced garments would be prized family heirlooms, appearing on, perhaps, a television show of Antiques and Collectables. But then such apparel, when outgrown, was passed on to another grateful young mother.

During the warmer weather in spring and summer (as there really were four distinct weather seasons back then), Ethel and Emma frequently spent long evenings taking in the air in the garden while work went on around them. The garden location, facing Rutland Street and running alongside Byron Road, kept them totally engrossed, looking as they did at the passing traffic, cyclists and pedestrians, talking ceaselessly. Initially they shared a wooden, ex-church pew, procured from I know not where.

Later, somehow, my Dad and Granddad obtained an all-black, wheeled Victorian carriage and installed it in the garden. A brougham carriage, perhaps?

A Lancashire Past

It had a double-ended folding roof, for protection from rain or hot sun, a feature not at all unusual back then. And there they both sat in their carriage, in regal splendour, cigarette smoke rising above their heads, Grandma constantly, but unavailingly, ordering Granddad to extinguish his perpetually smouldering bonfire.

Now, the site of all these memories is buried under a housing estate.

Another of my Grandma's sisters, Hannah, was a welcome if infrequent visitor. She was a gentle, kind, and loving Great Aunt, married to an equally kind and gentle husband, Fred. They were clearly a devoted couple. Married at twenty-one, for a while they together operated a fish and chip shop in Laneshaw Bridge. However, for whatever reason, they eventually returned to cotton.

In 1915, apparently pursuing more lucrative employment, Fred had left Hannah in their Nelson home and was working in Bolton. One day, suddenly, for Hannah, there was a tremendous shock.

Responding to a knock at her door, she found herself facing a posse of armed soldiers intent on arresting Fred as a deserter! It was a distinctly inaccurate description of that upright and honest man. Hannah quickly brought Fred home—both of them no doubt in terror. His army career was in the Royal Artillery (RA).

From inauspicious beginnings, Fred was to make a very significant and original contribution as a gunner. He was trained as a gun-layer, the vital member of a gun-crew. During this time, it was a function normally performed by a non-commissioned officer (an NCO). Fred was the sole private soldier in his battery to be considered sufficiently responsible and skilled to perform the crucial operation of gun-laying. The actual operation results in the gun being aimed at the correct elevation, range, and deflection to hit the intended target. And it was in Dover, in December 1915, that Fred's gun actually shot down one of the hated German Zeppelin Raiders. The weapon Fred was operating was a new three-inch gun specifically designed for anti-aircraft duties, and gun-layer Fred duly acquitted himself with honour.

It was the first Zeppelin thus destroyed. The doomed aircraft actually flew on some way before crashing into the English Channel with the loss of all the crew. The local dignitaries, led by the mayor, visited the battery to record the thanks and gratitude of the townsfolk. As a mark of their appreciation the mayor offered as a gift to the battery anything that the men would accept. The actual gunners, no doubt, had visions of, perhaps, a crate or two of the local brew. Instead, the unworldly battery commanding officer suggested that some gardening equipment would be very welcome! Uncle Fred and his mates were distinctly unimpressed. Spare time—digging!

Before long, and probably soon after the Dover posting, Fred served in France, where his battery came under German shellfire. Fred suffered perforated eardrums. Infection followed and, much worse, tubercular conditions developed.

On leaving the army, Fred was advised not to return to mill-work for medical reasons. Instead it was directly recommended that Fred seek outdoor employment. He took up cleaning windows, which clearly was a sensible move for him; he ultimately died aged seventy-nine.

Fred and Hannah had a son Tom and a daughter Edna. Their children, my contemporaries, helped produce this illuminating, significant, history of their Granddad, my Great Uncle Fred. Possibly connected to the importance to him of the open air, Fred's idea of relaxation was to keep some beehives. It was Great Uncle Fred who introduced me to a sweet passion I still enjoy on occasion to this day.

Taking me by the hand almost eighty years ago and duly kitting me with protection, he showed me the industrious bees entering and leaving the hives, and most importantly, the honey-packed combs, all the time talking quietly to the bees. 'Now then, lasses, this is Jim; he'll noan bother you, so doan't you bother him.' Apprehensive, I clutched Fred's hardened but gentle hand, anticipating the promised treat.

That's where I learned about delicious comb honey—sweet sticky bliss with the comb to chew afterwards. Much better than any chewing gum! I still, whenever possible, but sadly now having to contend with decreasing availability, treat myself to a small piece of honeycomb, remembering with warmth Great Uncle Fred and him introducing me to his bees.

Hannah and Fred's warm, friendly and welcoming temperaments also led them into socially conscious activities. At regular intervals, as many as five of the six Walker sisters, with husbands, would gather at their home, all greatly enjoying a typical Lancashire event, a potato pie supper, in their crowded terraced home.

Families were very important to these Walker women. Family values, decency, and consideration for others were passed on by example to the younger generation.

I can recall a significant occasion when I received one such lesson. Snow had fallen; our yards and paths had been cleared by Dad and Granddad.

Along our street lived a solitary pensioner. Handing me, aged about eight, a brush and a shovel, it was suggested that I go to Mr Trigg's house, clear him a path to his lavatory and to his coal shed and then make sure that his fire was burning. It was designed to be an early lesson in social responsibility and exercising consideration for the less fortunate.

A further example of the kindness of Fred and Hannah came with the outbreak of World War II. They opened their door to, it seemed, multitudes of evacuees. On one occasion they welcomed a desperate mother with seven children! As proof of their warmth to the strangers, one of their house guests is still in regular contact with the family sixty-five years afterwards.

Sadly, like the garden we cultivated and the seating there, shared by my Grandma and my Great-Aunt Emma, Hannah and Fred's house in Corporation Street is no more.

The adjacent allotment where Fred's bees lived is also gone. Both have now been flattened to make a car park for today's symbol of modern life—a supermarket. And a rotten swap it is.

Bands, a bear, and the community

The low level of activity in the cotton-mills continued up to the mid-1930s in reflection of the national depression—although the citizen army of World War I had fought on a promise that after fighting such a savage war in appalling surroundings they would return home to 'a land fit for heroes'. The reality was a great deal worse. In the cobble-stoned streets of terraced houses like Oak Street and Cleveland Street life was a continuing struggle. It was an appallingly familiar sight in the 1920s and early 1930s to see groups of itinerant former service men, some still wearing the remnants of their previous service clothing, playing on limited instruments; it was sometimes jazz music, occasionally popular tunes, and sometimes even some of the war-time songs. They were unemployed, playing for coppers or even just for food, among the working-class communities familiar to them. And despite their own struggles, my extended family and neighbours all, somehow, managed to find a few pence or perhaps a meal to share with their fellow men.

Unbelievable though it will now seem, I actually saw on our local streets a former soldier accompanied by his 'partner', a dancing bear performing to tunes from a penny whistle. A land fit for heroes indeed.

To illustrate the abysmal treatment of these 'heroes', and the low level of worker's incomes, coupled with the scarcity of work, we can consider the case of my Dad's elder sister, Florrie. She and husband Fred (Senior) had produced four children.

As a direct result of his war service, Fred had died in 1933, leaving Florrie alone to raise their four children, aged five to twelve years. A grateful government rewarded my Aunt Florrie with a widow's pension of ten shillings (fifty pence) per week.

The eldest son, Fred, was blessed with an exceptional brain. In the then selective system by examination when aged ten for a Lancashire County Junior Scholarship leading to a place at a grammar school, Fred had been an outstanding success. Additionally at that time there was an additional scholarship offered by the Emmott family of Laneshaw Bridge. The Emmotts—originally spelt d'Aemott—arrived in England with the Norman conquest.

From their estate, with an Elizabethan mansion on Haworth Road, they offered a scholarship to Colne Grammar School for any particularly outstanding local pupil. Fred more than filled that requirement; he was offered both scholarships. Sadly, from her pitiful income, Aunt Florrie was utterly unable to support Fred through higher education.

The Emmotts are no longer the local squires. Emmott Hall was demolished soon after World War II. At that time, a working man lucky enough to be employed in the cotton industry would be earning about £2 to £3 per week. So of course the family and the community rallied around to help Florrie to supplement her meagre earnings gained from cleaning the homes of the more affluent. But Fred was to be denied his chance. The cost was too high.

Shortly after the death of his father, my cousin Fred, aged fourteen, joined the labour force. Employment for school-leavers was difficult to find. Despite his demonstrated mental capability, the only job Fred could secure was in the warehouse of a local wine-merchant. In 1936, he was in the very first group of local drivers to pass the newly introduced driving test. He thus extended his usefulness to society as a driver. How absolutely wonderful for a lad capable of the highest intellectual attainment!

The outbreak of World War II provided the opportunity for him to make a contribution appropriate to his intellect. He was quickly called into the RAF, where for the whole war he was involved in RADAR development at the Daventry site of the original ground-breaking experiments of this electronic miracle.

At about this time, my own family wanderings began. We children were unaware of the reasoning behind our nomadic lifestyle. Somehow it did not appear to influence our development, and we always seemed to keep close ties with the family group wherever we were living.

Although as children we were unaware, both Dad and Granddad were increasingly involved in trade union affairs and local politics. There can be no doubt that they were influenced by the struggle of the working class to achieve decent conditions for their families. Both of them were members of the 'Twisters and Drawers Union'. Both also began to take an active part in politics.

At that time the Co-operative movement had a vigorous political wing, which attracted my Dad particularly. In keeping with the family standards and ethics, my Dad also regularly attended Worker's Educational Association (WEA) groups. He firmly believed in the principle 'Knowledge is power'. Political activity was an interest that played an increasingly important part in his life for the succeeding thirty to forty years. But, soon, his attachment to the Co-operative movement was supplanted by increasing involvement with the Labour party at official level.

And, predictably, at a very minor but practical level, my sister Sylvia and I were recruited to the cause, helping at local election times, folding leaflets, stuffing envelopes, exit-polling, collecting pennies at fund appeals and so on. But, inevitably, events moved to a more serious level.

In 1935 there was a general election. With our help and support, possibly aided by one or two others, Colne elected its very first Labour party MP. In a straight fight, Sydney Silverman defeated the

Liberal party candidate Lynton Thorpe—Uncle of the unlamented Jeremy.

Photograph 13 shows my Dad in a pose for some party function of the time. Photograph 14 is a picture of the author taken about the same time—a grubby, cheerful urchin at Park Junior School.

It is clear that politics was playing an increasingly important role in my Dad's life. Sydney Silverman was, for a brief spell, a frequent visitor to our home, although change was afoot.

Dad's politics, I hasten, were definitely not at the expense of his young family. Whenever possible we were taken into the countryside and encouraged to develop the love for the outdoors he so passionately felt himself. My brother and I particularly both shared his commitment to the countryside, and in turn have passed to our sons this undying need to be in the open air.

Being built on the Pennine Chain, it was inevitable that Colne was very hilly. Of particular significance was Tum Hill to the south of the town. The derivation of the name 'Tum' is possibly with the earlier use of the hill as a tumulus—an ancient burial mound.

There was also probable occupation of the hill as a Roman fortress. Nearby, at Caster Cliff, there are vestiges of an ancient fort and Roman influence. To infant eyes the hill was enormous, but in truth it rose to approximately 1,000 feet. It was of course a severe enough challenge for my first ascent for my Dad to have to carry me up on his back.

The flattened plateau was a favourite location for grasstrack motorcycle racing in the 1930s. Such excitement: the noise, the spills, the smell of the Castrol 'R' lubricating oil in my nostrils. On another such excursion, I was quickly hustled away from a noisy crowd of working men, almost certainly unemployed, involved in something I did not understand and something my Dad did not approve of—cockfighting.

At a time now when we are advised that the rat population is reaching almost plague significance and is of real concern in food production, I can look back to radically different times in this matter.

During my childhood it was common to see groups of men, again probably each one out of work, accompanied by motley collections of terriers and lurchers, sometimes with air-rifles, ferrets secreted in pockets.

Probably for modest charges they roamed the district, eliminating rats in local farms, under hen coops and anywhere that rodents were a problem. There certainly was then no question of rats being allowed free range in Colne and district. The local land owners and gamekeepers probably took a more jaundiced view of such a service! It is certain that game and game birds also were spirited away during ratting; they were hard times but even the underclass had families to feed.

More about wanderings

At the time that Tum Hill and district played a part in our lives we lived briefly in the steep Exchange Street leading down to the South Valley region of Colne. While living in Exchange Street, we briefly attended the nearby West Street Junior School. It was a totally unmemorable experience, apart from juvenile hysteria at the names of two of the teachers—Miss Pepper and Mrs Salt.

At the bottom of Exchange Street, in the valley, ran the River Colne. Historically, the river is the source of the name of our town. When my Dad was young it was a typical Pennine hill stream: fresh, sparkling and clear. It was full of bullheads, sticklebacks, loach, minnows and spotted beauties—trout.

A generation later it was nothing more than an open stinking sewer. Upstream, two tanneries and various other factories had been allowed uncontrolled access to the river to take away their detritus.

It was not, in the 1930s, an area in which children could be allowed freedom to roam, as we were encouraged to do. The countryside was our more normal, open playground.

Whether as a direct result or not, we were soon living in Sunny Royd Terrace, attending Christ Church School. The very name of Sunny Royd Terrace hints at an elevation in status. In truth, it was a terraced house immediately adjacent to the tram shed. The limited public transport in the towns was still dependent on the rumbling, noisy, jolting and uncomfortable electric tram, housed in the cavernous buildings adjacent to our street.

The continuation of our terrace, Heifer Lane, was rather steep, considered far too dangerous for trams to descend. Instead there was a safer, linked, descent to the rear of our house, down a specifically constructed gradient, known, of course, as 't' tram lines', connecting the tram sheds with the main road to the villages of Cottontree, Winewall and Trawden.

It was also of personal convenience. In the village of Cottontree there were cotton-mills, at one of which, Standroyd, my Dad worked for a time. For a brief spell, during my lunch breaks from school, it was my job to walk down the tramlines to the mill with my Dad's heated dinner bowl, wrapped in a towel and carried in a wicker shopping basket.

I would have been aged about six when I was given this early introduction to a place of work. The clatter from the weaving shed adjacent to the quieter preparatory area where Dad worked I found both frightening and fascinating.

The smiling welcome from the women operatives I remember fondly. It was a feature of life that was to be repeated many times as Dad's place of work changed, with the fluctuations of trade in the cotton industry, and where I continued to visit him at work. I was, invariably with smiles and a wave acknowledged by the working women. As an indication of the fluctuations of work in the cotton industry at the time, during his thirty years of life in that industry my Dad worked in no less than twenty-two different mills.

The house in Sunny Royd Terrace was the first home that Dad set out to buy, sometime in about 1932. Trade must, briefly, have been encouraging. But, for whatever reason, our domestic equilibrium was not to last. Our mother was inclined, for preference, to sample 'the good life', relative to the more practical and sensible standards of my Dad's side of the family.

For whatever reason, she suddenly collected the four children and, independently, moved us all to an address in Nelson. We children were, of course, completely in the dark. We had no idea what was happening. I do recall that I could turn a corner at the end of a street and there would be my smiling Dad, crouching down and hugging me tightly, but not living with us. Why?

Our new address was near to Barkerhouse Road. I was enrolled at the Walverden School, of which I recall absolutely nothing. I suppose events had traumatised my child's mind. I only knew that I saw my Dad very infrequently, and I missed him and the wider family desperately. Domestically, life was chaotic; a coterie of 'Aunts and Uncles', all total strangers, flitted through our juvenile lives, day and night. The provision of food assumed a low level in adult concern. For the first time real hunger entered our lives. It was not a home.

Nearby I recall a quarry from which was extracted clay, the source material for local brickworks. Briefly, it diverted young minds from our chaotic domestic circumstances.

We revelled in the delight of free, uncontrolled, gravity-impelled rides in the tubs, down from the extraction-face after work had ceased for the day and the night-watchman were 'otherwise engaged'. Concerns with health and safety now deny today's children such dangerous, squealing delights. But without doubt in our case it was a diversion from domestic trauma. Equally, without exposure to danger, how can children develop a healthy respect for it?

This desperate time, spent in the mid-1930s in Nelson, would, almost certainly, be prevented today. Despite occasional relapses, today's social care provisions for children are a great deal more pro-active.

For we Foulds children, help was at hand, from, of course, the wider family. My Dad's repeated, quiet, unobtrusive visits to see his children had more practical objectives; he was slowly building up a reference catalogue of movements and dubious personalities associated with 'our home'.

Eventually, he worked out a rescue plan. His younger sister, Mary Alice, had recently married. Her husband Jim Tomlinson was from local farming stock, although he preferred other work. He drove a heavy lorry for Feathers, a local company offering both wagons and coaches. Jim's brother, Frank, remained in the family farming business, where, thankfully, he had access to a small van.

With the coast clear, the three of them made a nocturnal, forced entry into our 'home'.

We four children had been left unattended while our mother was away on personal pleasures. Worse still, we were all locked in bedrooms. Thankfully, it was summer time; there was no need for any unguarded open fires. Our meagre clothing was hastily collected. All of us, with belongings, piled into the cramped van where we were driven away to a secure home.

I suppose that in today's enlightened times, our rescuers could be hauled before the courts for kidnap, or some such demeanour. What they did was magnificent, a triumph of human concern, family love and decency. They totally transformed our lives. Their action left we children with a debt of gratitude that could never be repaid, except perhaps by the subsequent actions in our lives Whatever we four children subsequently achieved in our lives only became possible because of our timely rescue from a situation that was potentially catastrophic.

And our destination? We were all spirited away to 4 Fern Street, Colne, where were already resident our concerned Grandparents, the loving Ethel, and the practical James, in a terraced house of two-up and two-down'. They shared the property with Aunt Mary Alice and her husband Jim Tomlinson. Aunt Mary was a hairdresser, using the 'front room' for her salon. Married only very recently, their contribution in welcoming an invasion of an adult with four children can only be described as heroic. Photograph 15, taken in the Isle of Man, shows Aunt Mary and Uncle Jim on their honeymoon in 1933, only a year before the upheaval in their lives.

They shared their bedroom with my two sisters while in the other bedroom, in two double beds, slept my Grandparents and my Dad, with his two sons. Those houses had rooms with a maximum size of about fourteen square feet. The sleeping arrangements have to be imagined.

The two relatively newlyweds were quite magnificent. As I matured and the realisation dawned of what the family had sacrificed in making a welcome home for my Dad and his brood I was indeed humbled. I saw it as a true display of love and family devotion.

Of course, the cramped living circumstances could not be allowed to continue indefinitely, and duly the necessary changes were made, as we will see. But first we turn to a discussion of the re-establishment of civilised behaviour.

The Primitive Methodist Chapel, with the football team captained by my Dad, enrolled us into its congregation, plus the Band of Hope, anti-alcohol body. Sundays took care of our religious teachings, and moral principles were instilled on Monday evenings at Band of Hope classes. *Jesus Wants Me for a Sunbeam* was the clarion hymn of Mondays.

Attendance at both bodies was studiously noted by a 'star stamp' for each visit, recorded in individual cards we all carried to the chapel. At the end of the church year, prizes were awarded for one hundred per cent attendance. Sadly I was not a dedicated attendee at either

Church or Band of Hope. Somehow there frequently seemed to be other diversions of greater interest; I was an emerging free spirit.

One such diversion from Sunday church attendance was the overnight appearance at the Skipton Road—Byron Road crossing of some magical lights that seemed to be able to alter their colours in a regular sequence, totally without any human intervention. I stood there transfixed, time and destination forgotten, watching these lights: red, red, yellow, green, yellow, and red. What little traffic there was seemed to obey these lights. It was a new invention that nobody had told me about. My presence at Sunday School Church would be totally forgotten; I stood gazing for the full period normally spent at church and returned home lacking an attendance stamp. No reprimand was forthcoming at home.

I suppose my family recognised, even at this early stage, that mine was an enquiring mind. That free spirits were to be encouraged was a principle of our upbringing.

Improving circumstances: a notable event

It was probably part of a family plan to try to blot out recent events in the minds of we children when, quite out of the blue, a family outing by motor car was organised.

Uncle Jim was employed as a coach and lorry driver. No doubt through his employers he arrived home after work at lunch time on one Saturday driving an enormous, shiny, black limousine. (Consequent no doubt of another of Henry Ford's pronouncements, all cars then seemed to be painted black.) There never had been a car like this one. To my juvenile eyes, it really was enormous. It was able to seat the extended family of five adults and four children in some comfort.

On Sunday morning, bright and early, with generous food provisions packed into the boot and all possible clothing loaded, we set out on my very first car journey. It was quite magical and unforgettable. With Uncle Jim and Dad sharing the driving, we left Fern Street to pass by places I had barely heard of, on roads which by today's standards were empty. Barnoldswick, Gisburn and Trough of Bowland in turn were all left behind us. Until, before long, the warm, golden sands of the River Kent estuary at Arnside on Morecambe Bay came into view. There were jugs of tea at 6d each, picnic-sandwiches made from home-baked bread as well as cakes similarly produced. We enjoyed our very first occasion of paddling in the sea. We engaged in beachcombing, searching for articles of value, and we went shell collecting. It was an utterly memorable delight. And there was more to come.

Leaving Arnside behind, via Grange over Sands, we travelled on to the Lake District. Here there was more magic awaiting us; we travelled by ferry across the quite gigantic Lake Windermere. How absolutely thrilling it was in the car and on a boat sailing across such a big lake, so much more enormous than the familiar reservoirs back in Colne.

I have no recollection of the journey home. We children were no doubt exhausted and asleep, but we knew that our loving family had treated us to a day full of memories to cherish. As I write I am recalling events of almost eighty years past, and the recollections are still treasured.

In the same period, and no doubt with the same sense of family concern, my Dad and some of his sporting cousins decided to take a trip to another far-off place, Leeds. Perhaps it was a period of more unemployment, with time to be filled. The objective was the Yorkshire County Cricket Club ground at Headingley, where the England team were to play Australia in the fourth Test match. I was taken to the ground on an auxiliary cycle seat fastened to the crossbar of my Dad's bike. In truth, I was probably too young for such a trip, although the family intentions were of the highest.

I have no recollection of the journey, or the company. The match was not sufficiently exciting for me. I do recall a very stern reprimand from my Dad. It was nothing physical, that was not our family behaviour, but my attention-seeking and inevitable wanderings were a distraction for the adults from important events on the field. The star of the Australian side, Don Bradman, was the major attraction. He was a member of a strong team that included people like O'Reilly, Grimmett, McCabe, Hassett and Brown.

The England team, equally strong, included such cricketing luminaries as Hammond, Hendren, Leyland, Wyatt, and Bowes. Much more importantly for our contingent, the England team also included a representative from 'our' family.

My Great-Grandmother's maiden name was, of course, Verity. During the 1930s the outstanding left arm spin bowler for England and Yorkshire was a name's sake, Hedley Verity. However distant and detached the connection, the Lancashire arm of the Verity clan rallied in support of him. Sadly, neither he nor any other England bowler could curb Bradman's assault, as he plundered the England attack for 304 runs during the day's play. A slight consolation was that Verity did capture three Australian wickets.

Apart from Bradman and Verity, I remember virtually nothing of the game. It should have put me off cricket for the rest of my life. Thankfully, it did not. Over the following years, and under changed transport arrangements, I returned to Headingley several times. One particularly notable occasion will be featured in due course.

On the domestic scene, having, during family wanderings, attended three other schools, I returned to my former Park Junior School. No particular fuss was made. I simply re-joined the class I had deserted, with the same pupils—children of less adventurous and nomadic families than my own—and got on with my formal education.

In retrospect, it seems to be indicative of the less controlled nature of schooling apparent to me then. Perhaps I over-simplify, but I am sure that education today is a great deal more centrally controlled and a great deal less flexible than was the case during my childhood. Is it better, I ask?

Photographs 16 and 17 record a very special event in the Walker side of my family from 1935 when my Great-Grandmother celebrated her eighty-fifth birthday. There she sits, with her cake bearing the requisite number of candles, in the back yard of her final home, 58 Oak Street. To celebrate the event, all of her six daughters and her two sons, with spouses, assembled. Photograph 17 shows them all, looking remarkably hale and hearty, well presented for the occasion and, remarkably, all aged in their fifties and sixties.

Of their spouses, only Great Aunt Florrie Whittaker's is missing. This is, surely, a remarkable photograph: an eighty-five year-old matriarch, together with all of the eight children she had delivered into the world. She had raised them all in a period of severe deprivation for the working class. For the times, the celebration of an eighty-fifth birthday was in itself a very notable achievement. To have shared the event with all of her eight children is astonishing. What a remarkable event this was. It is not, I fear, the kind of picture that, now, would be very likely to appear. Today, families are fragmented, often scattered worldwide. I am thankful indeed that so much of my formative life was spent in such a warm, close, family-centred, community-conscious, welcoming, and loving environment.

There was, of course, a supporting party at which the wider family was present—in numbers. Needless, of course, to record, I myself managed to dispose of my share of the cake, plus a sip of my Great-Grandmother's celebration Tarragona wine. And is that not an extraordinary detail to recall? Sadly, I was soon to lose my Great-Grandma. Within very few months of her eighty-fifth birthday celebrations, she passed away. For me, there was to be no more singing to her and no more of the usual barley sugar rewards from her 'pinny-pocket'.

Change of address

The cramped living conditions of No. 4 Fern Street soon came to an end. Uncle Jim and Aunt Mary Alice were able to resume life appropriate to a recently married couple on their own. Late in 1935, the remaining seven occupants of Fern Street moved to a much larger house at No. 17 Rutland Street.

Apart from the additional space provided, it was conveniently adjacent to Park Junior School attended by Sylvia, Brian and me together with many cousins. After school, we frequently enjoyed playing street games together.

The Rutland Street house was certainly a great improvement over Fern Street in terms of capacity. So much so that for the Christmas period of 1935, the occupants increased from three adults and four children to four adults and eight children! The extras were Dad's elder sister, Florrie, widowed, with her four youngsters.

The significant memory of that episode is the sleeping arrangements for the juveniles. There were two double beds, one with four boys and the other containing four girl cousins, all arranged head to toe alternately. There was not much sleeping; there was a lot of giggling and recrimination. With so many energetic youngsters together for that memorable Christmas break, maintaining control and interest and avoiding mischief exercised adult ingenuity. In those days, long before computers and iPods, physical activity was the norm for children.

Ignoring the cold—or perhaps to warm the juvenile forms, we were sent outdoors, into the back lane, to take part in normal games of the period—hopscotch, rounders, and primarily, skipping. The 'party-sized' rope was turned by the adults with us eight youngsters bobbing up and down to one or other of our favourite skipping chants.

I particularly recall an oft-repeated song based on the Generals of the Boer War. This refrain must have been passed on generation to generation or how could we conceivably known of:

> 'The War. the War, the blooming War,
> Has turned my wife insane.

> From Kruger to Majuba
> She's the Transvaal on the brain.
> We went to christen our first child,
> Last Sunday week we tried,
> The Parson said, "What's this child's name?"
> And my old gal replied:
> "The baby's name is Kitchener, Carrington,
> Methuen, Kekewwich, White,
> Cronje, Plumer Powell, Majuba—'"

and so on, for another fifteen or twenty names.

Quite what the point of the game was and who was the victor I no longer recall. But what is certain is that the physical effort involved kept us occupied, drained us of surplus energy, and briefly gave the adults a break.

Rutland Street sloped steeply from the main Colne thoroughfare down to Byron Road. It was the scene of an accelerating descent by the author on a borrowed bicycle, terminated by a head-on collision with the gable end of our terrace, a painful re-arrangement of facial aspect and a wrecked cycle. The ownership of that bike is now a mystery.

The event appeared to persuade my Dad that my cycling education should become something of a priority for him. But a problem: I did not own a cycle. The Skipton Road Methodist connection provided a solution. There, Saul Clitheroe, one of my Dad's friends, handed over his own cycle. He had moved on to a motorcycle. His old pedal-cycle was in a neglected state, having been left outdoors in rainy Lancashire for some time.

But my resourceful Dad set about restoring the wreck to something approaching its former condition. First, Dad stripped it to component parts, eliminating rust by vigorous scraping and emery-papering. It was then re-painted with brilliant red enamel. New drop-handlebars were added as well as white, celluloid, Bluemels mudguards, new bearings throughout and a new chain. It was quite the transformation;

by the time my Dad had finished it resembled a boy's dream of a cycle. There was one cloud on the horizon, though; it had only one gear. Steep hills were a penance. But, it was my pride and joy—until stolen about five years later.

A temporary driver's mate

Despite their heroic early behaviour when their domestic bliss had been devastated by the arrival of four boisterous children, Aunt Mary and Uncle Jim were not to be blessed with a family of their own. Cruelly, while still a schoolgirl, Aunt Mary had suffered a severe accident. It didn't prevent her from becoming a local champion swimmer. Sometime in the early 1930s I watched her swim the width of the nearby Lake Burwains—about half a mile. She, separately, also swam the mile or so length of Burwains. But, sadly, the earlier accident meant that she could not bear any children.

Maybe Uncle Jim felt his loss more closely than Auntie Mary appeared to show. Certainly, he made me his driver's mate. With him I travelled widely in Lancashire and Yorkshire. The experiences of sitting by his side while collecting woollens from Bradford and Halifax or any of the scattered towns and villages of the West Riding gave me an invaluable bump of direction that is still with me now. Some afternoons, released from school, I would find Uncle Jim's wagon waiting for me in Rutland Street. Off we would go on a journey of, for me, delight and discovery.

At that time, there was still, in Barrowford, a flour mill, powered by a water wheel. All the grinding and power-lifting of the sacks of grain came from this slowly turning and splashing wheel using the River Pendle Water, passing through sluices. This I suddenly remembered a few years later—as will emerge.

It was, to me, magic, watching the slowly rotating wheel, the bags of grain hoisted, mysteriously, to a higher level without anyone apparently doing anything to help.

But even more thrilling for me was a visit to the Docks. Then, the Manchester Ship Canal basin at Salford was quite unbelievable. Great big ships in the middle of a city! How could that be? It was a phenomenon too difficult for me to grasp.

In my understanding, a canal had barges, at the time pulled by horses on the nearby Leeds-Liverpool canal. But these were ships, in Salford. A puzzlement, but for a boy 'from the country', a revelation.

The first time we took a load to the Liverpool Docks it proved a different type of education. Uncle Jim had successfully driven to the correct dock. For me this was a triumph in itself; the whole complex was a tortuous bewildering maze. But when we did arrive at our allocated spot it soon appeared that our problems were just starting. There was a queue of wagons; we were near the front, and yet others kept passing our waiting wagon. Eventually Uncle Jim left his seat. Before shutting his door he told me to stay in the wagon and to not to leave it until he returned. If anything occurred that I did not understand, I was to sound the horn and to keep on doing so until he re-appeared. Particularly, I was to keep my eyes on the load of cotton bales behind the lorry-cab.

And off he went. He soon returned, without an explanation for his absence. When I tried to investigate, he simply tapped his nose and uttered one word: 'Ganger'. Within only a few minutes we were unloaded. Young though I was, I understood that sometimes adults behaved mysteriously, and small boys must keep quiet.

What had happened on that initial trip was the standard routine on all subsequent visits. But, for me, sadly, my time as a driver's mate soon ended. Uncle Jim blotted his copy book, and I was denied a very pleasurable, instructive, pastime. The normal time for me to join the wagon was after school in the afternoon. To my delight I was leaving school at midday, and there waiting in Rutland Street was Uncle Jim's wagon. He had come to take me on a quick trip to Skipton. Unfortunately he failed to inform anyone at home of his plan. When I hadn't arrived for my dinner at 12.15 p.m., adults began to wonder. Always a hungry child, my mealtime appearances during school terms were reliable. By 12.30 p.m. there was real concern at my home. Our eventual return at 1.15 p.m. produced a storm of relieved anger on Uncle Jim's head.

For me, the punishment was unbelievably disproportionate. Subsequent wagon trips became extremely rare.

Games and pastimes

I cannot recall an occasion as a youngster when the current childish whine of 'I'm bored' was uttered. As I remember, we simply did not have enough time available to cram in all that we wanted to do: cricket, football, the open countryside, cycling, ball games in streets empty of traffic, and always our garden, needing work. Primarily, of course, we had our allocated domestic duties and training. Between the elder three children, the chore of fetching the routine shopping was organised.

At that time, the Co-operative shop met almost all domestic needs. It was even possible to order deliveries of coal, which later appeared at the back door by horse-drawn cart.

Twice each year the dividend on all purchases, from ten to twelve and a half per cent, was collected from the Co-op head offices in Albert Road. The accumulated dividend was invaluable in balancing so many domestic, family books. Just about the only necessity not available from the Co-op was milk. This was routinely delivered daily on a horse-drawn cart by the farmer who actually had earlier milked his herd. The milk was held in steel churns, secured in the back of his open cart, and served into one's own jugs by a handled measure dipped into the churns. Health and safety?

The cooking skills I learned from my Grandma were more than adequate for me, forty years later, to personally take over the kitchen of our own eight-bedroom hotel. And, additionally, cleaning and laundering. But that's a later story. We boys were also very committed to flying kites that we made ourselves. The raw materials of cloth, string, and stiffening ribs were all free-issue from family members variously involved in textiles. The flying-field was usually the football ground. There was fierce rivalry among the lads to achieve the highest kite. And it was on a kite-flying day that I witnessed a quite astonishing event. The exact date was 26 May 1936. There in the sky to the north, a very few miles distant, was the majestic, silver, cigar-shaped *Hindenburg* German airship.

Although distant, it was an inspiring sight. Returning on a transatlantic flight from North America, the enormous dirigible had diverted from the planned route to complete an act of memorial. During the Great War, there had been a German prisoner of war camp between Keighley and Bradford. Sadly some prisoners had died while in captivity and were buried in a graveyard at Riddlesden. Among the airship's passengers was a relative of one of the deceased prisoners. Apparently of sufficient authority, he had arranged for the airship's return route to pass over Riddlesden to allow him to drop a memorial wreath at the graveyard. In that diversion, I was treated to the only sighting of an airship in my life, and I have never forgotten the impression it created. In those days the limited arrival overhead of a buzzing biplane was an event. To actually view, even from a distance, the silver bulk of an airship was unimaginable.

As we lived so near to open countryside, we of course spent long hours outdoors. In the nearby King's Beck, a clear, unpolluted stream, were limitless caddis, grubs, and insects, food for the resident fish population. There was all the normal fresh water tiddlers, sticklebacks, loach, bullheads, and minnows. And, in season, breeding lampreys.

A small fishing net cost a penny, and a jam jar with a string handle was all that was required to transport home the day's catch. A typical fishing party is shown on Photograph 17a. The author is nearest the camera, and Sylvia is the nearest girl, intent on a stickleback's capture. This picture, taken by a friend of my Dad's, was an unsuccessful entry in a national newspaper competition.

This little stream was, significantly, the main tributary into the linked trio of reservoirs, terminating in Lake Burwains, which supplied water into the nearby Leeds-Liverpool canal. Two of these reservoirs were stocked with trout by the local fishing club.

King's Beck was the spawning ground for the trout. Inevitably trout fry occasionally became unintended captures in our little nets. The outcome could be catastrophic for the net, incapable of containing a struggling six-inch monster.

In the unlikely event that we actually captured a trout, it became an al-fresco snack. We boys always carried matches; a 'den' was usually constructed and a fire of twigs was a standard requirement. Any unfortunate small trout we captured we would wrap in dock leaves and then quickly bake it in the embers. It was a light snack that was very promptly eaten. Supplied with a picnic, we could spend a whole day by and in the beck and in the nearby woods. We would climb the trees, seeking bird's nests, and in spring, gather bunches of the bounteous bluebells, later to sit in jam jars on windowsills at home, their scent filling the house. Bored? Never!

During the countryside wanderings of our childhood, there was neither need nor money available for the currently ubiquitous bottles of expensive branded drinks carried by almost everyone. Then we were lucky to have accessible, clean, clear, unpolluted sparkling water in ancient sandstone drinking troughs for animals at the road-side. Sadly now they have disappeared, occasionally replaced by galvanised troughs. The original items have become prized fashion adornments, available at high prices in the burgeoning garden centres. New owners are totally unappreciative of their origins and oblivious to the many grateful children who for sixty, seventy, eighty years slaked thirst from them, in addition to the animals they provided for.

All that was necessary, prior to drinking, was to sweep a hand across the surface to remove resident water-boatmen or pond-skater beetles, to enjoy a satisfying drink of cool, clear water. No need for Pepsi or Coca-Cola or an energy drink then. Now, the nation's water may be considered clean and drinkable, but it is often unpalatable, carrying a whiff of chemicals. It is a travesty of that which generations of children would drink from roadside animal troughs. It's called progress; health and safety, probably.

In spring we spent hours in the open air in pursuit of what, now, is largely illegal and certainly shameful. Almost every boy of the district had at the time a collection of bird's eggs. My brother and I were no less culpable. We had what was considered a very fine representative collection of the local birds. Two of them I can still nostalgically recall, one with amusement and the other with disbelief.

A mute swan had built its nest in a disused, wooden boathouse, on a local, neglected, small boating lake. Swans, in the protection of their nests and family, are determined and potentially dangerous birds. Although only aged about seven and nine at the time, Brian and I were determined to get one of the eggs that the pen bird was incubating.

On the wall of the boathouse were some disused oars. Keeping an eye on the birds I grabbed two. One I used to fend off the threatening cob, who was circling, and to guard the entrance to the boathouse. Meanwhile, using the other oar, Brian levered the pen off the nest and grabbed an egg. We both beat a hasty but triumphant retreat.

In retrospect it was very foolhardy. Small boys are unaware of danger, and we were typical boys.

Our Dad was of course perfectly well aware that his sons were a mischievous and wandering pair. By nature I was the leader, with Brian content to follow. But, oddly, when authority called at our home, somehow it was generally Brian who had overstepped the mark. And so it was in the matter of the second, notable egg, which still rests in my memory. Brian had been out separately; I arrived home to be greeted by a triumphant brother. He'd found a wild goose nest, *and* he'd got one of the eggs! A triumph indeed. But it was extremely short-lived.

There was a knock at the door, answered by our Dad. He sought his sons, accompanied by Mr Sutcliffe, a local farmer who had been directed to our home by other boys. He had come in search of an egg taken earlier that day from a domestic goose nest on his nearby farm. Shame-faced, Brian produced the egg he'd found. There, plain for all to see, in scrawled pencil on the shell, was the date that the egg had been laid, scratched on by Mr Sutcliffe. I cannot recall the outcome of this episode—apart from the two of us being forbidden, briefly, to leave the house without first acquiring specific permission. The modern expression I suppose is 'Grounded'.

We spent much of our time wandering in the King's Beck area. Our elder sister, Sylvia, found for us in that stream bed our first sandpiper's nest of four eggs. Our sister knew her brothers well. Although we were committed collectors, we had a self-imposed morality code. We never took for our collection the total contents of any nest we found; we were not nest robbers. The exception, of course, was in early spring, when eggs represented breakfast. Then, the birds would always produce a second clutch. In today's climate, what we were doing would be wrong.

Now, the fields where we found abundant nests are often silent. The wheeling pairs of peewits in the skies above all the pastures of our childhood are now a rarity, and I am saddened that my Granddaughter can never know what she is missing, in the joy of discovering and merely observing the natural beauty of a concealed bird's nest, with contents.

Over the King's Beck was also where I saw my first dragonfly. It was a wondrous sight, quartering over the stream. It was a beautiful, iridescent blue, with wide, shimmering, beating wings. I was intent on capturing this beauty and I followed it, up and down, skimming back and forth, over the stream, until, ultimately, it settled on the trunk of a willow. Carefully, I crept up on it and quickly clamped my small hand over my quarry. What a shock for me! The wretched thing bit the palm of my chubby hand. Startled, my hand withdrew, and the dragonfly soared away. Another lesson; I never again tried to catch one of them.

It was also in the King's Beck region that Brian and I learnt, to our painful cost, about the consequences of interfering with wasp's nests.

We had been watching these black and yellow striped flies entering and leaving a hole in the bank of the stream. For whatever reason, Brian decided to poke a stick in the hole and to give it a stir. The outraged wasps swarmed out to the attack. Within seconds we were both coated with the wretched things, stinging and stinging as we fled.

I don't recall exactly how many stings we received, but we were a very sorry pair before we managed to escape the wasps' revenge. It could be said that, henceforth, we would give wasps a wide berth. As we will see in due time, nothing could be further from the truth. These wasps would get their comeuppance.

In the 1930s there were two golf courses in Colne. One is the existing one on the eastern edge of town, on the Lothersdale Road. The second one, a nine-hole course that is now defunct, was situated on the outskirts of Laneshaw Bridge, off the Haworth Road. This was grandly called the Colne St Andrews Golf Club. For a brief spell in the late 1930s I tried earning a few coppers there as a caddy. The venture was soon consigned to history. For a boy, the weight of a bag of golf clubs, of even the limited size then in use, generated more shoulder pain and fatigue than could ever be compensated by the shilling a round. The limited exposure to the game led on to other significant interests. The first was the significance of the expression 'hole in one'. I learned that such a feat gave the golfer concerned brief kudos. The counter-balance was the cost of a round of drinks in the clubhouse at the end of the round.

The second hole at the St Andrews club involved a drive across the Colne Water, to a 'blind' elevated green about fifty feet above the tee. The situation lent itself to repetitive juvenile humour at the expense of superior adults. The putting surface was situated in a bowl that gathered the balls onto the green. Behind the green there was a small copse of shrubs to hide mischievous schoolboys.

A concealed lookout watched for players leaving the previous hole. When all the party had driven to the second green, one of us would creep quietly across the putting surface, take the ball nearest to the flag and drop it into the cup. From our hide we suppressed giggles at events on the green. For a brief spell, the 'hole in one' successes at the second hole at St Andrews Golf Club soared—as did the bar takings. Juvenile interest briefly occupied, without the latest computer game.

The second point of golf interest arose based on the value of the golf ball itself. Unskilled players inevitably drove balls into the rough. Much time was spent seeking errant balls. At the end of the day, it became for me a potentially rewarding exercise to find lost balls that we may not have, previously, sought very diligently.

The cost of a new ball then was 10p to 20p. I found that I could sell retrieved balls back to willing golfers at about a quarter of that price—an early demonstration in 'recycling'.

Moving again

Early in 1936 we were once again on the move, from the rented property in Rutland Street. The family owned house at 2 Elm Street had become available. A significant reduction in outgoings was the first welcome benefit to our adults. Unlike Rutland Street there was no rent to pay. It also offered even more space than the place at Rutland Street. The two main ground-floor rooms were all at least twenty feet square. Additional to a generous separate working kitchen and three bedrooms there were two enormous attic rooms, matched by cellars of the same size.

Most impressively the bathroom was sumptuous, relative to our earlier facilities. The fittings, all blue and white, were willow-patterned, and, most notably, the lavatory basin—a flushing lavatory, at last—had to be approached up three steps! In truth, it was a throne.

By our established standards, it was unbelievably opulent; the electric power provided improved illumination. The cotton industry's fortunes recovered, and with it our family circumstances. There seemed to be more money in the house. About this time, Granddad significantly demonstrated his claimed support for women and their right to be provided with labour—saving domestic equipment. Photograph 17b is a contemporary picture of him.

The first relevant purchase was an electric washing machine. It had powered rollers, a central agitator, and an emptying pump. It was, in fact, for the time, an extremely advanced design. Made by the Scales Company in Keighley, it cost £23.62-about the equivalent then of eight weeks' wages for a skilled cotton worker. Not only did it lighten the domestic load for my Grandma but, additionally, my Aunt Florrie and Aunt Mary came weekly with their laundry. It was a practical demonstration of one of Granddad's basic principles—'Wimmin shudn't hev ter labour.' At the same time arrived another 'mother's helper'—a Hoover vacuum cleaner. We children were soon well-versed in its operation. It was part of our domestic education and preparation for life.

It was not solely labour-saving equipment that appeared. The provision of entertainment was included. Previously we had had a wind-up gramophone and a 'wireless'. At that time, before the universal installation of domestic electricity, a radio—always known as a wireless—was necessarily powered by a wet-cell accumulator. (It is the small cousin of today's motor-car battery.)

Dependent on usage, these batteries could quickly be drained. Each town had a facility where exhausted batteries were taken. The exchange service was operated for, I think, a shilling for each battery. The need to renew a battery was four to fourteen days. At our newest home, this system was soon consigned to history. The house was equipped with mains electricity. A wonderful new invention was purchased, an HMV radiogram. It was a relief to be able to hear a complete programme without the worrying thought that the battery may be exhausted before the programme had ended.

As well as our established favourites like *Children's Hour* with Derek McCulloch (Uncle Mac), and the early nature and wildlife broadcaster Romany with his dog Raq, we learned about commercial Radio Luxembourg and 'Ovaltineys', a Chidren's association. "We are the Ovaltineys", the song we all sang. Ovaltine, a bedtime milk drink supposed to promote slumber. Nothing more than an early exposure to the delights and pressures of the advertising world.

Culture was also catered for, with our own children's newspaper, an Arthur Mee production, as well as, of course, membership of our local, Carnegie, public lending library. All the family were avid readers. From age seven we changed our library books weekly; it was more frequently if the librarian was sympathetic to boisterous young readers.

The Silver Jubilee anniversary of the rule of King George V and Queen Mary was celebrated in 1936 by a royal visit to Colne. The town children were assembled at a saluting base at Hyde Park Corner, the junction of North Valley Road and Vivary Bridge. The event failed to capture my interest.

Of much more significance to Brian and me was the Jubilee cricket match between Colne and Nelson at their Seedhill ground. At the time the professional cricketer for Colne was Amar Singh, a member of the All India national team in the days before partition.
He was a tall, slim, athletic and talented all-rounder. But Nelson had, as their professional, in my resolute opinion, the world's best-ever all-round cricketer, West Indian Learie Constantine. He was awesome in his talent.

Brian and I simply had to watch this match. A blazing hot day, the ground was packed. A chalked bill-board circulated the pitch, announcing the gate-takings. The exact amount I forget, but it was near to £250. The entrance cost for an adult was 6d, and for boys, much less. Significant numbers of urchins, including us two, knew where entrance without paying was possible. The crowd was in excess of 10,000.

Memory of the game has faded, but I do recall that boys were allowed to sprawl on the grass. Somehow, we were late arriving, and even the grass was packed full. We were totally unable to find a spot with a view of the cricket. A typical schoolboy's solution came to us. Brian was always prone to nose bleeds. We agreed that I would give him a gentle tap on his nose. And, in modern parlance, there was 'a result'. Sympathetic adults soon cleared a space on the grass on which to lie down was Brian. For us, soon, there was a good view of the game.

The HMV radiogram was, of course, an enduring success. Apart from the BBC broadcasts, we now had access to extraordinary radio stations like Hilvershum and Hamburg and many others. Most impressively, we could pick up shows from places much further distant than Europe, leading to an especially memorable treat for the author.

The American world heavyweight boxing champion Joe Louis defended his title against a Welsh boxer, Tommy Farr. The bout took place in 1936, in Madison Square Gardens, New York, at about 2 a.m. in Britain.

My Dad brought me down from bed to listen to the commentary. I remember the broadcast as being variable in volume, the sound tending to ebb and flow like the tide, and with sibilant overtones. But then, what an unexpected thrill: listening to events from across the Atlantic Ocean as they happened. The sound of Farr's Welsh supporters in the 50,000 crowd, singing, as only the Welsh can, *Land of My Fathers*, was loud enough to drown the Americans' support. Farr was, reputedly, 'unlucky'. He was the first opponent to face Louis and fight the, then, fifteen championship rounds. It was a memorable and exciting event for me. Surprising, too, as neither my Dad nor my Granddad were dedicated boxing fans.

Animals, pets, fishing, provisioning

During one of our country wanderings, Brian and I were delighted to find what we thought were two baby rabbits, lying concealed in a grass tussock. They were actually leverets, as normal, left by the mother hare while she went about other matters. Delighted, each of us stuffed a baby 'rabbit' under our shirts and hurried home.

The enormous, dry, but crucially, unused cellars at 2 Elm Street were, to us, ideal for raising these creatures. There would be no need for a hutch; they could have free-range living conditions. So, avoiding adult attention, we made what we thought were appropriate living provisions for our new pets. A bowl of milk, some rolled oats, and a few green leaves from the garden took care of their food. Various bits of timber, some linoleum offcuts, created hiding places. And, somehow, we managed to make use of an old coat for a bed. We were well pleased with our charges and the arrangements made for their comfort. Of course, the adults were unaware of the new members of the household.

I cannot recall how long the arrangement lasted, but the animals soon doubled in size. Clearly our organisation could not last; it came to an abrupt end when Grandma, unusually, went down to the cellars—and hastily retreated. Dad was called. 'Jim,' said Grandma,' 'you'd better get down into the cellar. There are some rats in there.' The truth emerged. There was retribution for the young. 'Grounded' again. And without any juvenile intervention, the rabbits disappeared. It was to the table they went, of course, although nothing was revealed to me and Brian.

It was not our only attempt at rearing wild creatures. Soon afterwards we were returning home from another adventure in the countryside and, walking along one of the local country roads, we came across a sad sight. At the roadside there was an adult road-casualty—a hedgehog. Snuggling up to the dead mother were two babies. Obviously they could not survive alone, so we picked them up and carried them home. This time, adult support was forthcoming. With milk feeds from an eye-dropper and careful weaning by Grandma they survived and developed in their cellar home. Lucky animals, these two! We named them Amos and Andy, two well-known characters from an American radio programme we heard on our new radiogram.

Before long they were considered ready for an outdoor existence, and off they went to their new home in the garden. Hedgehogs are a distinct asset in any vegetable garden.

These two made a welcome contribution in their control of ground-pests. The sound of them chewing a slug, on the edge of dark, was both awesome and disgusting. They stayed with us certainly over one winter before, to our regret, wandering off to a better home.

The important question of food arises again. By today's standards the food we all ate in the 1930s could best be described as wholesome, nutritious, and unadventurous. Creditably, it was, almost exclusively, home-made. Pizza, pasta, and curries were totally non-existent. Rice was for milk puddings. What is absolutely certain is that the children did not go hungry. And equally probably, the adults forfeited their own needs for the young.

Typically, my Dad made the principal dietary decisions. What we ate could certainly be described as varied. There was fruit and vegetables—from the garden mostly, as well as poultry, meat, fish, game, and eggs as already mentioned. Additional purchases of meat rarely included a roast. The cheaper cuts of meat were for stews, Lancashire hotpot, and potato pie, typically. Broth was made with a sheep's head for the base, with garden vegetables and dumplings made from a piece of butcher's suet and then grated into the bowl of flour. Atora, a commercial mixture of beef suet and flour, in the distant future.

After the broth had disappeared, the residue meat, tongue, and brains, stripped from the sheep's head, were made into a delicious terrine. It would no longer be acceptable, of course, under our modern, sad food-policing controls. At the time, there was an excellent tripe-dresser's shop in Colne. Their cheap products were a part of our occasional foods. Stewed tripe and onions was a delicious and filling meal. I haven't eaten any for ten years and then it was in rural France. I have, again, been deprived. But rarely in my childhood. Breakfast, generally, was porridge, made of oatmeal, rolled oats, or maize meal. Occasionally it was eggs.

Grandma was an excellent, industrious, productive baker. She made bread, biscuits, sad-cakes, and pastries like apple pies and custard tarts. She also made ginger parkin and a flavourful, family, spiced mixed-fruit loaf called vinegar loaf, named thus because it contained some of that condiment in the mix. It was a recipe that my Grandma taught me, and the recipe is still with me. Bread and cakes were not a usual purchase except on Saturdays. Then, at about 4.30 p.m., my Dad would head off into the town to the markets, in search of unsold produce at knock-down prices. At the time, there was a busy, open-air, Saturday market in Dockray Street known as the Jew's Alley.

Dad's purchases could never be predicted; they could be anything from a bag of wholemeal loaves to a score of herrings. A carrier bag of crabs I particularly recall. It was all perfectly edible food, which, in the days before the universal use of refrigerators, could not be sold on the following Monday. And an afterthought: there was for a time an evening hawker, calling his wares around our streets. He specialised in a fruit that is now a rarity.

It was a small, sweet, delicious, red-skinned banana, grown then in the Canary Isles. It was sold in complete stems of eighteen to twenty-four fruits. No doubt it was another supermarket accountant's casualty.

Unadventurous our food might have been, but there is no doubt that we were well fed. What we had was typical food of the working class. And any suggestion of juvenile hunger was solved by a slice of home-made bread and jam.

The adults, generally, ate moderately, even frugally. I particularly recall one of my Granddad's favourite meals when he came home between shifts; he enjoyed a pancake covered with minced meat and onion gravy. Now they are available on supermarket shelves, called tacos, enchiladas, or perhaps tortillas. Of Mexican origin, they are a modern feature of supermarket offerings, in a packet, of course. I prefer the wholesome food of my past—my Grandma's offerings. Other exotic foods are now widely available from all corners of the globe. In our childhood, the only available convenience food was native. But then, even at the 1930s' price of fish and chips a bout four pence, they were a rare treat. The food we ate, produced and eaten at home, or al-fresco on picnics. There were no such comestibles as curries, sweet and sour, or kebabs. How on earth did we survive?

A particularly eventful period

About this period, for the first time in our lives, arrangements were made for a family holiday. It was to be a week in a Cleethorpes' boarding house. All nine members of the extended family were to go, to be transported by, again, a limousine, hired by Uncle Jim. Joy of joys!

Sadly, for the author, it was to be disappointment. The day before departure Dad took me aside and gently broke the devastating news that the holiday party had had to be reduced to seven. The real reason was never explained; there was just the firm directive that my Dad and I would be staying at home. To ease my sense of betrayal and disappointment, Dad told me that he had other plans for us. He had made some arrangements that would have far-reaching effects on my life of leisure pursuits.

One of Dad's friends had donated to me his redundant fishing tackle. Dad would take me and introduce me to the Isaac Walton brotherhood. It was the roots of a passion only terminated by arthritis a few years ago. But for sixty years or so I was hooked. As in due time was my son and now my Granddaughter.

The nearby Leeds-Liverpool canal was the site of the introductory fishing trip, in particular where the outflow from Lake Burwains enters the canal, known locally as the Byshakes. On the day, hungry and obliging small perch ensured a day to remember.

Of course, the fishing tackle was soon shared with my brother, a common joy throughout our lives together. Initially, our trips concentrated on coarse fishing offered by Lake Burwains and the nearby canal. Dependent on the availability of cycles our range could extend along this waterway to East Marton or nearly to Skipton. Not much of our catch was edible—perhaps perch or an escapee trout. But as our tackle improved bigger fish swam into our ken.

Lake Burwains contained pike; at that time the usual method of fishing for these predators was by the use of a small, live-bait, fish, a cruel method that is now illegal. But then, using small carp or goldfish surreptitiously extracted from local mill dams, our success in catching pike was notable. A six-pound pike, stuffed with garden herbs and oven-baked was a very welcome diversion from routine fare. (For a brief diversion into an explanation of carp and goldfish in mill-dams, the motive power for cotton-mills was by steam-driven piston engines. After the steam left the engine it condensed and was passed into a storage dam. All mills had them; the warm water in these dams was then passed back to the boiler and recycled, repetitively. In the warm dam water weeds rapidly grew and, unchecked, could clog the system and stop the engine cycle. To counter weed growth, all such dams contained a population of carp-family fish. Their diet was the weed; they could grow very rapidly in such advantageous conditions. Their only predators, small boys and herons, were both in their turn vigorously discouraged by vigilant 'engine tenters'.)

The real limitations to our fishing were financial. At a time when our combined weekly pocket money was about 8p, a trip to Burwains cost 5p. The Lancashire River Board licence covering the canals cost about 15p per year. Clearly, our finances dictated that the canal was our more usual location. When the sun rose so did we, packing the tackle and some emergency rations, and either walking or cycling to the water. When the sun waned, we headed home. Then, quite by chance, through a joint stroke of serendipity, cunning, and enterprise, there was a radical improvement in our finances.

The East Lancashire coal field of that time extended to nearby Burnley, where, in the 1930s, there were still, I think, four active pits. The miners released into daylight sought the open country for fresh air and relaxation. A significant number used to regularly fish Lake Burwains. Brian and I made 'fishing friends' with one of these miners. I have never forgotten the man; named Jimmy Topping, he was a 'ripper' underground at a Burnley pit. For his job, he spent his working life on his side, in seams of coal often as narrow as eighteen inches, ripping at the coal face with a pickaxe. I recall him

A Lancashire Past

removing his shirt, in the summer, exposing the blue, scarred results of his troglodyte life. There was not much mechanised coal recovery then. He was, to us, also notable for his extraordinary food. All he ever brought with him was half a dozen Bury black puddings, which he often shared with us two, eaten cold! He also shared with us his cigarettes.

By now, as a result of shocking adult examples, aged only eight and ten, we were both committed smokers. Jimmy would extend to us his Woodbine packet with the offer, 'Here, hev a coffin nail. They'll kill thee, tha knows.' Sadly, it was a very long time before the truth he spoke became accepted reality, based on medical proof.

As a result of their lives predominantly spent underground, these pitmen had little opportunity to procure their fishing bait. Jimmy frequently arrived at the lakeside without any bait. We, of course, met his shortages. Generously, he also paid us. Soon, whenever he planned to visit Lake Burwains, he would send a postcard and place an order for delivery at the lake. From these beginnings, Brian and I developed our own bait-supply business, regularly circulating around the lake selling our stock. From the garden we got different types of worm; from King's Beck came caddis, grubs and minnows; from local mill dams came illicit carp and goldfish. Most significantly, we had jointly developed a reliable and safe system of collecting wasps' nests. It was sweet revenge for our earlier suffering. Wasp larvae are an almost irresistible meal for any fish, and they were then eagerly sought as bait by anglers.

For three or four years we had money to finance new fishing tackle and permits. Crucially and stupidly, at the weekend we could afford a packet of 'Senior Service' cigarettes-5p for a packet of twenty. Shocking! Jointly, we established what could best be described as a 'nice little earner'. It allowed us to extend our tackle significantly, and to fish further afield, sometimes in pursuit of trout in local streams. And now it can be confessed we also joined the ranks of poachers in the protected waters of the Colne Angling Club. Devious boys! The clean, unpolluted upper reaches of the River Colne Water, particularly between Laneshaw Bridge and Wycollar, increasingly attracted our widening trout-fishing interest.

At Laneshaw Bridge, in the 1930s, there was an active cotton-mill. For the operation of their steam-engine, a tributary of the Colne Water was diverted. At the end of the working day, this diverted stream was directed down a flume back to the main river. Briefly, it created a maelstrom where trout gathered to feed. With careful timing, it was for us a very productive fishing spot.

In summer, the local children dammed the main stream in order to create their own swimming pool. As dusk fell and the swimmers departed, the pool then became a rewarding fishing location. Then, in the Colne Water, the normal stream depth was twelve to eighteen inches, even up to the higher reaches. Removable trout inhabited the length of this river, upstream of Cottontree, to even Wycollar. To the detriment of us anglers, the local Water Board, in the nearby catchment area hills, placed an extraction bore for drinking water. The inevitable consequence was that river flow reduced to a trickle compared to that of our time. There are now no sizeable fish; the water insects they feed on now are very limited.

As earlier indicated, the River Pendle Water was used to power the grain-mill at Higherford. Like the Laneshaw Bridge cotton-mill, when the grain-mill's day ended, water diverted from the main river held in the associated coffer dam was released back to the river.

As boys, we had no knowledge of such arrangements. Our ignorance resulted in, for us, a frightening, and potentially fatal, situation.

Brian and I were illegally fishing for trout in this river, in Barrowford, downstream of the mill. At the position there is a weir-cascade, at the bottom of which we were blissfully fishing. At the end of the grain-mill day, the volume of river-water suddenly, massively, increased. The previous, friendly, flow over the lip of the cascade became a torrent, soaking the pair of us to the skin. Although that was bad enough, I suppose that the outcome could have been much worse. Lacking appreciation of the situation we never again fished at the bottom of that cascade.

Fishing for trout, sea-trout, and salmon would, over the coming years, increasingly dictate our angling interests in many other, distant, waters. For the time being, our fishing remained local.

Additional to the trio of reservoirs ending with Lake Burwains, there were also two others built to service the canal. The many reservoirs in our locality were necessary because the canal stretch, between Nelson and Barnoldswick, lies at the peak of the whole canal length. Each time a boat passed through this stretch, the locks at each end had to be opened, draining away a lock-full of water to lower level. This emptying effect meant water had to be continuously replaced from reservoirs.

Of these two further reservoirs, the one at White Moor was stocked with trout and bailiff-controlled. Of no use to us, then. The second, smaller stretch of water nearby was called Old Ebby's. In it there was a healthy stock of roach and perch. More importantly, it was unsupervised and therefore cost us nothing. Together with two other boy-anglers, Wallace Berry and evacuee John Waters, we decided to establish our own private fishery. Adjacent to the Colne Golf Club, there was a disused quarry half filled with water.

We decided that here was the ideal spot for our fishery. Old Ebby's reservoir, three miles distant, provided our stock. Over the next few months we laboriously transported about 100 small perch and roach to the Castle Road quarry.

Although we never ourselves tried our own fishery, we later heard that our work was a distinct success and was enjoyed by later young anglers. And for a while, it kept four boys usefully employed transferring stock fish to their new home. Bored? Absolutely not!

In our childhood days, canals were still being used for transporting appropriate cargo. The changeover from horse-drawn, to propeller-driven, barges was not yet complete.

When canal-fishing, we preferred the horse-drawn type. The canal—bottom contents, stirred by the passing boat, created a brief spell of feeding by the fish. The under-water propeller noise had the reverse effect.

A pleasant and not unusual diversion was occasionally created by the sound of a water-vole dropping into the water. In calm water, a vole swimming past, under the surface, was an attractive sight. Its fur contained a 'coat' of buoyancy air bubbles, giving the animal a surprising silver sheen.

Occasionally, a rare kingfisher would perch on a rod tip—provided we kept still and quiet. And if we were more than usually reluctant to leave the canal-side, it was also common, as daylight faded, that the bats would leave their roosts in the nearby Foulridge tunnel. Their skittering flight, in search of moths and flies over the water, often involved amazing, rapid changes of direction in order to avoid our rods. We hadn't, yet, learned about the echo-sounding technique employed by bats in flight—the principle later adopted in the development of our air-defence RADAR system.

A day on the canal bank quite definitely was not all about fishing. Our ultimate reluctant return home, no doubt a relief to adults, was just occasionally accompanied with a gentle reminder of the time.

While we lads continued to keep ourselves occupied with as little impact as possible on adults, our Dad's involvement in politics had been intensifying. At this time, although us children were not aware of the reasons, Dad had, unusually for him, been absent from home for odd days. On one particular occasion he spent a full week absent, at a 'conference' at Llandindrod Wells. Soon, the reason for the change in his behaviour became clear. His politics had shifted significantly to the Left. He had joined the Communist party. He became a frequent speaker at local meetings and rallies. Letters to the editors of various publications mushroomed. In truth, he had become a distinct 'Burr under the saddle of The Establishment'. Inevitably, he was elected Secretary of the local branch of the party.

Additional to our normal *Manchester Guardian*, the *Daily Worker* was now delivered. From time to time it became one of my chores to deliver the latter newspaper. The total readership in Colne was about fifty, spread across the whole town. Although the papers had to be collected from Colne Railway Station at 6 a.m., it was rare for me to return home before 8 a.m. In icy winter conditions, it would be even later. But, it didn't seem to do me any harm, apart from frequent winter spills from my bike and the painful spasmodic chilblains.

I again stress that our Dad's diversions did not affect his family relationships. We still went on cycle rides, or a picnic, or just a walk in the country, and, necessarily, the garden. And, crucially, we also were more than adequately cared for by our Grandparents.

On 20 February 1937, my Dad was responsible for me being afflicted by a disease that is still with me. On that date, for the first time, he took me to Turf Moor football ground.
Burnley was to face George Allison's mighty Arsenal FC. At that time, Arsenal were the most feared team in Britain, with a panoply of internationals: Male, Hapgood, Joy, Copping, Crayston, Alex James, and Ted Drake. In contrast, Burnley was in the then second division. But, since that day, I have been a dedicated supporter of the Clarets. It is a disease without antidote other than the regular, if remote, support.

Burnley FC was an original, founding member of the English football league. Despite the noise emanating from the nouveau riche Johnny-cum-lately clubs like Manchester United, Arsenal, and Chelsea, nothing can detract from Burnley's proud boast to have been in at the beginning of the very first national football league in the world.

Fading past glories, perhaps, but pride in achievement earned by a very select few The honour of founder membership of the very first football league football in the World predominantly Lancashire clubs.

On that famous day in 1937, the ground was absolutely packed. The crowd was in excess of 50,000. In the health and safety concerns of today, the blood runs cold at the very thought of football grounds then and the unthinking disregard for the safety of the supporters. The Burnley ground was typical. There was a small terraced area in front of the single pitch-wide stand. The remaining three sides of the ground consisted of nothing more than the accumulated detritus of the many local Lancashire boilers of nearby cotton-mills. Ashes piled up and compacted into a bowl offered standing room for crowds, with a few intervening tubular crash barriers as protection for surging crowds. (In March 1946, at the Bolton Wanderers FC ground at Burnden Park, the threatened tragedy occurred. In a packed ground, of similar construction to Turf Moor, an uncontained crowd surged off the banking, and the pitch boundary wall crumbled, spilling the tumbling crowd in an accumulating pile. Thirty-three supporters lost their lives. It was forty more years before all-seat grounds became law in the leagues where such crowds could be anticipated.)

For the Arsenal match I was hoisted onto my Dad's shoulders; otherwise I would have seen nothing. When the Arsenal team emerged from the tunnel facing me, apart from the diminutive wizard Alex James, they looked like giants. Comparatively, the Burnley players were pygmies. And duly, Burnley was brushed aside, thrashed seven to one.

I may have been shattered, but the virus took hold. Still today, seventy years later, the first football result I seek on Saturdays is the one involving Burnley.

Now, in these days of billionaire football club owners lacking any real affiliation, massively indebted clubs, and millionaire players significantly from overseas, the proud traditions of the Burnleys of this world are forgotten. But they are certainly not forgotten by me or by a band of similar traditionalists. Football then may have been played at a slower pace, but support was tribally based. It had nothing to do with celebrity.

About this time, my Dad had changed his place of work again. At the bottom of Phillips Lane in Colne was a cotton-mill owned by a

Bradford company, Cawthras, where he then was employed. It was commonplace for me to visit him at work, sometimes to share lunch. This mill was on the edge of the town, almost rural. In fact, on a visit there I heard, in 1937, for the very last time, the call of a Corncrake. Now, throughout our islands, these shy, elusive birds can only be heard in Ireland and in the highlands and islands of Scotland. I still treasure, mentally, the bird's rasping call that I heard seventy years ago in rural Colne, never since repeated.

The year 1937 was significant, also, as the Coronation year of King George VI and Queen Elizabeth, the Queen Mother. A commemorative photograph was organised at Park School; photograph 18 shows the author—still grubby, still smiling.

Also that year, although oblivious of family pressure or expectations, there was for me the county junior scholarship for selective entry to grammar schools. The scholarship was the great social escalator of the day; through the grammar school system there was an opportunity for escape from wage-slavery in the mills and workshops of industrial Britain.

The brightest lad in Miss Tierney's 'top' class was John Scott. His family worked the 'Old Earth' farm near to the football ground. As well as being very intelligent, John was also highly strung. On the morning of the scholarship examinations I was walking alone along North Valley Road, heading for the test centre at Lord Street School, when, astonishingly, running towards me, away from the school, was John Scott, almost in tears. He'd forgotten the pencils, eraser, and ruler we'd all been given at our school for use in the examination. I tried, unsuccessfully, to persuade him that he would be able to acquire replacements at the exam centre. But, distraught, he carried on running to his home—more than a mile distant. On such a bizarre event, a complete life was determined. When John did return, late, he was in no fit state for the test before him. He was unable to demonstrate his true potential; he 'failed the examination'. I prefer to think that the system failed him.

Aged fourteen, he joined the workforce as a farm labourer. We retained spasmodic friendship until, with me aged sixteen, I also started work. In the intervening period I spent much time as an unpaid, but well-fed, helper on the Hob Stones Farm where John worked. Conveniently, the farm lands bordered Lake Burwains—handy for fishing. The farmer's wife was unable to cope digestively with almost all foods. The one thing she could consistently eat was fish of any kind: perch, roach—despite the copious bones—or pike from the lake. For me, briefly, it was an income.

Unlike the unfortunate John, I and six others of Miss Tierney's class were allocated places at Colne Grammar School. Scholarships were worth eight guineas per term—about twenty-five pounds per year—and were equivalent to about seven weeks' wages for a skilled worker in the cotton industry. Also, unlike my older, cleverer, cousin Fred Senior, I was able to take my allocated place at the grammar school primarily because, in my home, there were two wages supporting the seven occupants.

My Grandparents, and my Dad, were no doubt pleased with my success, but no particularly public fuss was made. I expect that my Granddad was gratified that at least one of his descendants now had the opportunity to lift himself above the drudgery and wage slavery of the then, normal, family working lives. Independently, my Dad quietly signalled his pleasure by presenting me with a 'prize'. It was an LMS railway holiday run-about ticket, providing one week of unlimited travel on the network at a cost of ten shillings (fifty pence).

I suppose it was another opportunity for Dad to develop my independent streak and at the same time open my eyes further to the world beyond Colne and district. Possibly also, there were other travelling plans in mind, as will emerge in due time. I promptly, unaccompanied, took the train from Colne to Llandudno. It was an extraordinary day trip for a ten year-old. The time spent travelling could be thought disproportionate, but I was pleased at the evidence of my growing independence.

Probably with me exhausted by the trip, 'my' ticket was used the next day by my sister Sylvia and a friend. Alternately, thereafter, we used that ticket to the full—every day another adventure. I went to Scarborough, and I went to Southport. (At the latter I visited my cousin Ethel Senior, working in service in one of the 'big houses' there. I also demonstrated my callow background by ringing the bell at the imposing front door and demanding to see my cousin. I was haughtily directed to the servant's entrance. It was another of life's confusing lessons.)

I also re-visited the Lake District, on a trip to Lakeside and Bowness, including a boat trip between the two places on Lake Windermere. Included on the sail was a diversion to view a macabre notice, sticking out of the water, announcing the site of the recent fatal crash of Captain George Eyston during an attempt on a world water speed record.

A sum of ten shillings was never, ever put to such use as the ticket that Sylvia and I shared in 1937.

Another unexpected present for me as a reward for the scholarship came from my Granddad's brother, Alfred. He was a very spasmodic visitor and had made little impact on our lives. He did not, somehow, seem to be quite as family-conscious as the other, Walker, side of my family.

Alfred was a committee member of Colne Cricket Club. He arrived at our house with a magnanimous gift to me of a season's membership of the cricket club. For a while at least I would not have to sneak into the cricket ground without passing through the turnstiles. And, even better, for a while Alfred also took me with him to matches, at strange places like Todmorden, Haslingden, Rishton, and Bacup.

At that time the most notable professional cricketers in the Lancashire League were ex-members of the 1933 touring West Indian team.

Learie Constantine I mention separately, in detail. Additionally, playing in the league, was the fearsome fast bowler, E. A. 'Manny' Martindale, and the brilliant stroke-playing, high-scoring batsman George Headley. George was known as 'The Black Bradman' At the time, the most prolific scorer in International cricket was Don Bradman—a white Australian. Fifty years later, Headley's Grandson was to play for England.

And then there was the left-arm spin bowler Ellis Achong. He was responsible for the establishment of a descriptive expression still in use in cricket today, regarding a particular method of spin-bowling.

It followed from his dismissal in the 1933 Test matches of the English, upper-class amateur and autocratic selector G.O. Allen. Achong bowled Allen out with a delivery that had spun in the opposite direction to normal. As Allen left the crease, he was heard to mutter, 'Well, fancy that, bowled by a ****** Chinaman!' Achong was in fact half Chinese and half Carib, born in what is now known as Guyana. This 'wrong-un' ball from a left-arm spin-bowler was thereafter always known as a 'Chinaman'. It is for me a warm memory to have seen these pioneers of West Indian cricket wearing their flamboyant maroon caps with palm tree, sand and blue sea badge. The world was shrinking.

About this time, my cousin Donald entered the workforce. Like his brother Fred, he was also unable to secure a decent job equivalent to his undoubted talents. He became a junior farm labourer—an unpaid employee, 'living-in' with the farmer's family.

Initially, his only source of income was that which he generated for himself. The farmer allowed him a few day-old chicks, which were then reared with the farmer's own flock. Eventually, Donald was able to generate some money from the sale of eggs, and later, from the poultry itself. At length, the farmer, each year, would allocate Donald a brace of ram lambs from that year's crop. Raised with the farmer's flock, in due time they were sold at the local Auction Mart. Occasionally a bull calf would be allocated to Donald to rear and sell at the auction. During this farming apprenticeship, Donald began to share his life with a like-minded girl. Edna Whalley was herself a farmer's daughter.

Ethel, elder sister to Fred and Donald, had found similar, low-paid, work as a 'live-in' maid at the 'big houses' in Southport and Manchester. Clearly their combined contribution to the senior household budget would be miniscule. The best that could be said would be that someone else had the cost of their keep!

Fred and Donald were soon to join the Armed Forces, Fred serving in the RAF while his brother chose the Fleet Air Arm (FAA). Soon after the war, three of Aunt Florrie's children, with their families, left for Australia. Their move was sponsored by their father's brother Arthur. He had left Colne during the bleak 1920s. In Australia, the lack of formal education and training did not hamper progress. Both boys were natural entrepreneurs. Over many years all were able to develop a succession of varied, rewarding, and successful business enterprises. The intention was that, once established, the young people would arrange for Aunt Florrie to join them. Sadly, she died before this came about.

It was also around this time that I began to understand that my Granddad's finances were not solely based on his work in cotton. He was backing horses regularly.

But, crucially, he was definitely not a gambler. He was, in today's parlance, a professional backer. His wagers were, quite definitely, mathematically based.

I had for some time noticed that in the cupboard, near his living-room chair, he kept four foolscap ledgers. They in fact contained his accumulated store of horse-racing information collected diligently from the press, stables, trainers, owners, and jockeys—anyone who could help to build his store of equine knowledge.

Two of these ledgers recorded information about horses in steeplechases: 'ower t' sticks', as Granddad called them. The other ledgers contained information gleaned about horses 'on t' flat'.

In the evenings he would pore over the appropriate ledgers before settling on his choices.

His betting slips were very complicated, written in, for me, incomprehensible language: 'cross-doubles', 'trebles', 'each way', 'anything to come', 'on t' 4 o'clock at Wetherby' and so on.

His daily stake could be from £2 to £3, about the equivalent of a week's wages. But he was not gambling. He steadily made profits. It may only be tiny, perhaps a shilling or two, but he won consistently. He was a consummate professional, using his statistical brain to beat the odds. That is how he could afford to finance the purchase of a house to keep his family's living standard high and, yes, in due time to have money available to help descendants—like me through grammar school.

In Colne at that time, there were, I think, three bookkeepers who handled the local gambling. It was, then, illegal to gamble off-course—that is, not actually at a race-course. The bookies had agents in pubs, and clubs. In my Granddad's case, he went to the Social Club of his Twisters and Drawer's Trade Union. Allegedly, at the sight of Granddad approaching, bearing a betting slip, bookies would go pale and suggest that he take his bets elsewhere. But at a time when their usual punter would be wagering a couple of shillings, my Granddad's total of £2 or £3 was normally simply too tempting to ignore.

From his profits Granddad always managed to keep the family boat on an even keel. He was the family savings bank. Another of his favourite mantras was, 'Never a borrower nor a lender be.' Thankfully, where his family was involved, he didn't apply his own strictures. About twelve years after the above, my darling wife and I moved into our first home together.

With our accumulated savings we had been able to furnish the three bed semi-detached house, apart from a carpet in the hall and one on the staircase. Briefly we had bare boards, until shortly afterwards, in the January sales (when there really were such genuine events) a roll of carpet ideal for our needs was on offer—at £50. At the time that represented five weeks' wages to me. From his back pocket Granddad produced the money, to be repaid interest free, as I accumulated it. A few years later when my company offered workers' shares at face price, my Granddad's savings financed the full cost of £100. His advice about borrowing and lending did not apply to family. Money was always available, interest free, certainly to those who were making an effort.

Granddad's passion for the horses continued into his eighties, until his always weak eye sight became simply unequal to the clerical chore of collecting his data. Sadly, I failed to appreciate his genius with horses, or perhaps he was more tenacious than I appreciated then.

Just once, in 1959, with our first car, I was able to take him on a day's racing—'on t' flat' at Ripon. He was then aged eighty-four, still as sharp as a tack, as Photograph 18a shows—and he was still a determined smoker! He selected all the horses we backed, easily generating enough to finance the total cost of the trip and for us to return home with a profit. As I said, he was *not* a gambler.

A messenger boy

My Dad's political activities progressively became more demanding. I suppose, also, that we children were also developing and taking on more domestic responsibilities. This must have relieved him of some family concerns. In any case, we always had our Grandparents to watch over us. What did become evident was that my Dad's gradual development of my independent travelling capabilities was of increasing use to him.

His political activities were attracting attention. His letters to the Press, his public speaking, and his willingness to take a public stand in the name of the Communist party all clearly marked him out, in the eyes of 'authority', as an agitator to be closely observed. This, let it be noted, was seventy years ago, long before the present-day security surveillance. It seemed that he became suspicious that his postal deliveries were being opened before he saw them. Without alerting me in any way, he decided that, in future, significant mail could not be entrusted to the postal services.

For the next few years, I was used as a dependable messenger. I was totally unaware of the underlying motives. For me, it was simply another enjoyable adventure.

The principal correspondence and literature was sent to him from Manchester. Normally I travelled there via the X43 of the Ribble bus services from Colne to Lower Moseley Street bus station. I had three addresses to visit from which I collected packages. Thankfully I was never challenged. But occasionally Dad advised use of the train—perhaps a diversion from any observation. I suppose I was pleased to be thought sufficiently mature and reliable to be sent on such trips, without ever understanding the reasons, until many years later.

Personally, I enjoyed the opportunities to wander about Manchester and to gaze at the public buildings indicative of Manchester's then, significance, based on the cotton industry. There was the town hall, St Anne's square, the free trade hall, the cotton exchange, and the cathedral. Additional to fares, there was also a modest allowance for me. It was for food, principally, but it did also allow for rides on public transport.

I enjoyed exploring, and in so doing, developing an understanding of the city's geography, which in a few years' time would become of personal value. Then, my visits were of importance to Dad and equally, enjoyable to me.

Learie Constantine—a tribute

Returning from a Manchester trip by train, my feelings can be imagined when Learie Constantine, the cricketing God, entered my carriage. He was accompanied by another West Indian who I assumed also to be a cricketer, although he seemed older than Constantine.

They, largely, talked between themselves, but I was occasionally included in their dialogue. I don't suppose I made much contribution; I was probably over-awed. In any case, my home team was Colne.

Constantine played for neighbouring Nelson. There was to be no fraternising with the enemy!

It was some time before I learnt the name of Constantine's companion. He was, in fact, C.L.R. James, also West Indian, and resident in London. He was an eminent author, playwright, and social thinker and a force in the advancement of the Caribbean peoples.

The initial cricketing autobiography by Constantine, written in 1933, was denoted, 'With the assistance of C.L.R. James'. From his humble Caribbean roots, and with the guidance and help of James, Learie Constantine launched on a punishing path of education and self-improvement. On the day we shared the railway journey to Nelson, he was returning from evening classes studying Law at Manchester University. What he ultimately achieved is a shining example to any under-privileged person prepared to make appropriate personal effort. Constantine's Caribbean home was little better than a wooden shack.

When he first set foot in Britain with the initial, 1933, West Indian touring cricket team, he must have been astonished at the comparative living standards. He resolved to set about improving himself while simultaneously using his athletic talents to earn a living as a sportsman. When, in 1937, we shared that railway journey, he was routinely travelling to Manchester several times each week, to university study. His cricket prowess grew; although still 'only' playing Lancashire league cricket, he was, in 1940, Wisden's 'cricketer of the year'. He was appointed MBE in 1947, and in 1952 he joined the Bar in London. Following a spell in politics, and government back in the West Indies, in 1962 he returned to London as High Commissioner for the West Indies. He was knighted that year. He died in 1971, and he is buried in Hampstead.

From incredibly humble beginnings, what Constantine achieved, totally against the prevailing colour prejudice, was Herculean. He is the proof, if needed, of the triumph that human spirit can achieve against the worst of adversity. I am humbled to think that, over seventy years ago, I once shared a railway carriage with such a Titan—and even exchanged a few words with him.

J.W. Foulds

A culture shock: Colne Grammar School

On 20 August 1937, I began my secondary education at the grammar school. The Victorian building in Albert Road was the second school in Colne to be called 'grammar'. The original, tiny one, built by the town worthies in the eighteenth century, is still there in the churchyard of the St Bartholomew, parish church in Market Street. My generation was the first significant wave of working-class children to enter the Albert Road School. Financial limitations had previously excluded the children of local artisans from a deserved higher education—my cousin Fred.

The changes I experienced, from the small friendly primary school, were immense. At Park Junior School, the sense of community meant that there were literally no strangers. We were all known to one another.

At the grammar school, in a total of about 350, mixed, pupils aged from ten to seventeen years, I knew literally only the four boys and two girls with whom I had shared Park School. There, we had had six classrooms. At the grammar school there were about thirty classes. I was purchased the standard rig-out for a school uniform, with a new cap and blazer. The clogs we had previously worn were abandoned, to be replaced by the shoes only previously worn at weekends. There was a comprehensive range of sports kit for the gymnasium, for cricket, and for rugby—a heavy demand on family resources.

Although it was a mixed school, the sexes were separated into individual playgrounds. My classmates were the offspring of doctors, dentists, auctioneers, teachers, the Church, and—a very, very few—artisans, holding scholarships.

In the classes at primary school, all the teachers were responsible for tuition across the whole curriculum. At the grammar school, specialist teachers taught individual subjects, with frequent changes of room between classes. It was strange and, for a while, very confusing. Not all the grammar school teachers were welcoming. In fact they tended to the forbidding, exemplified by the headmaster. He had previously, in 1928, represented Britain at lacrosse in the Olympic Games in Los Angeles.

His prized Olympic blazer was worn as frequently as possible. A tall, aloof, glowering character, he would view from on high with apparent disdain us of the common herd.

Some understanding of him can perhaps be gained from the subjects that he personally taught to us juniors: the scriptures and elocution. Clearly, in his judgement, there were some rough edges to be knocked off us representatives of the lower orders. Briefly I formed a classroom friendship with his younger son, which also began to extend to him sharing my outdoor pursuits. Possibly under his paternal persuasion, it was a friendship of limited duration. Perhaps my Dad's public persona was also of significance.

Sadly, the allocation of a grammar school placement had unforeseen, occasionally painful, consequences. Educational separation at ten years of age resulted in my having to run a gauntlet through neighbouring gangs contemptuous of the exclusive grammar school uniform.

To minimise such confrontations, it became routine to vary the route to school. But, inevitably, battles were unavoidable. Arrival at the school in a distressed, dishevelled condition was by no means unusual. The official school response, possibly predictably, was unsympathetic. Maybe it was viewed as behaviour to be expected from us of the lower classes. No apparent effort was made to organise any official riposte.

Forty years later, in similar circumstances but 200 miles distant, my own son was compelled to face the same pack behaviour. Bullying, sadly, is a constant and recurrent phenomenon in even civilised societies.

In the 1930s, the emerging local, Colne and Nelson Rugby Club, had briefly played their matches on a farmer's field near to our home. My Dad had taken me to view this strange game, with noisy and vigorous young men chasing the queer, oval-shaped ball.

So when I arrived at the grammar school to learn that football was to be replaced by rugby, I had a rudimentary understanding of the game. I took to it with enthusiasm and some achievement. In due course, I played for the school's junior team as well as the Colts and the first XV. Our playing fields were along Barrowford Road, quite close to Cawthra's cotton-mill, where my Dad worked. No doubt with paternal pride, and without any notice to me, he left his work early on the morning that I was appearing in my first trial for a place in the Junior XV. He hid from view to watch proceedings. There was no fuss, no bother and only quiet approval at my selection.

My first game was against a public, preparatory school, Malsis, close by, in Yorkshire. My loving Grandma, considerate of the autumn chill, had knitted for me a pair of black, woollen mittens. While a revolutionary concept at the time, such are now favoured by many footballers and rugby players, particularly those from warmer, sunnier climes. My Grandma was a pioneer much in advance of things to come.

The vast majority of our games were played in Yorkshire: Keighley, Skipton, Bingley, Bradford, and in Halifax a total of three schools. In Lancashire, I can only recall playing Kirkham and the minor teams from Stonyhurst Public School. As a small, mixed-sex school, our fate was usually a defeat by opposition from generally larger and boys-only schools. The attachment to the game was probably salutary preparation for life ahead.

Perhaps the achievement and pleasure I derived from the game could be directly the result of our enthusiastic games masters. They were the antithesis of the majority of the teachers of intellectual subjects.

They were certainly more directly associated with their charges. One of them, W.G. Kellaway, was politically involved with my Dad—although possibly not so far to the Left.

His friendship with my Dad didn't prevent him picking me up and depositing me in a cold bath when I refused to take a post-match bath. We were not too burdened with hot showers in the 1930s, and

I was no Spartan. We had a bath at home, with hot water. Why be a martyr?

Family concerns

The year after my move to the grammar school, my sister Sylvia joined the workforce. Following a brief and unhappy spell retailing biscuits, she moved, almost inevitably, to the cotton industry. In nearby North Valley Road a small cotton-mill, J. D. Barritt, had attracted my Granddad. He was joined by Sylvia as his 'reacher-in'.

The function of preparing the cotton 'beams' for the weaving shed involved a tedious process of threading the cotton strands through a set of eyed-wires called a 'reed'.

Once installed in the weaving shed and in process, the reed raised and lowered the threads as the shuttle oscillated, carrying the weft cotton, thus creating the weave.

The reacher-in sat facing the loomer, passing in sequence the threads for the loomer to draw into their location in the reed. It was a mindless, boring job for an active, young girl. Soon, Sylvia moved on to the more demanding and rewarding work of 'cloth-looking'. This was a form of final inspection of the weave, correcting any remaining minor blemishes left by the weaver. It also included a process that, to me, seemed to be distinctly hazardous in a cotton-mill. Using a lighted candle, she expertly and swiftly passed the flame over the edges of the cloth bale, thus burning off any loose strands of cotton.

Cotton-mills were notoriously prone to fire. A few years earlier my Dad had roused us from sleep to view the conflagration of a nearby blazing mill. The sight and sound of the roaring flames I never forgot. To see my sister with a naked flame in a cotton-mill disturbed me.

In J. D. Barritt's mill worked three loomers and twisters, a highly skilled preparatory trade of the cotton industry. For me, it was always

J.W. Foulds

exciting to visit my Granddad there. Often when I visited, these three elderly men would spontaneously start singing while continuing their tasks. They created a wonderful a cappella harmony, and it was a joy to hear Johnny Greenwood, John o' Moses, and my Granddad, lacking any sort of conductor. The middle one of this trio, so named in ancient northern tradition, identifying John, son of Moses. (His baptismal name was actually John Thomas Hartley; he was noted and highly successful in local pigeon-racing circles.) Their singing repertoire included hymns, one of which particularly pleased me. From the non-conformist Sankey hymnal, it was entitled 'Only Remembered'.

Seventy-five years afterwards I was transported back to Barritt's Mill and my Granddad's 'group', on hearing a wonderful a cappella, Yorkshire, trio 'Cooper, Boyes, and Simpson' singing this very tune on a CD recording.

It is revealing to look back to the cotton industry of the period. At the peak of activity, about 750,000 people earned a living from the cotton industry. During World War II, the government appealed for increased output with the slogan, 'Britain's bread hangs by Lancashire's thread.' Now, the county is an industrial wasteland. To complete the family association with J.D. Barrit's, our cousin Jean Senior was eventually employed there. She, as my sister, started work initially 'reaching—in' for our Granddad before training as a weaver. Apart from our family relationship, Jean was also a close friend; our paths were closely interwoven until, post-World War II, she immigrated to Australia with her brothers Donald and Fred and their respective families. Even now, nearly sixty years on, we are still able to talk exhaustively by phone, she in Australia, me in Cumbria, remembering when we were young together in Lancashire.

Domestic activities continued, particularly in the garden. Later, during World War II, the government publicity machine urged the population to 'Dig for Victory'. Our family needed no such exhortation; we had been digging for our food for years past.

However, my move to the grammar school brought with it changes in our gardening routines. My school was about a mile distant; I had to leave home significantly before Brian and my sister Marjorie, who continued at the local Park schools. So each morning, before I left for school, it became my routine job to visit the garden and open the glasshouse doors and windows, particularly when the sun shone. Additionally, I was required to leave in the greenhouses buckets of water and liquid manure to warm during the day. When Brian left school in the afternoon, he then took on the task of feeding and watering the plants and, finally, closing the houses down.

Almost inevitably, divided responsibility led to disaster. I was returning from school for the day once when I was met by a highly agitated Brian. 'You're in trouble,' he said, 'you forgot to open the greenhouses, and all the plants are burnt to cinders!' It may have been a slight exaggeration, but, Oh Dear!

Deep gloom followed until Dad returned from work. Thankfully, he was able to partially salvage my damages. The foliage of the tomatoes, marrows, and cucumbers were certainly crisped, but mercifully, they were not beyond recovery, and the produce was unaffected. Apart from a gentle paternal admonition and a reminder of attention to duties, I survived for another day, to continue my gardening activities. Like the poor, always with us.

Brian and I continued our established social lives together, unaffected by our separate schools. We still roamed the countryside and went fishing together and jointly operated our bait-selling business. Until, suddenly, he was struck down by rheumatic fever.

Apart from the severity of this attack, we children were generally of good health. Certainly we all in due time attracted the usual childish ailments like mumps, measles, and chicken pox, but there was nothing of major concern. And certainly we created very little work for the local health system. Brian's illness was something quite different. It was, apparently, a very serious attack, one that was potentially fatal. His bed was brought into the living room, to maintain a steady temperature. Each night, one of the adults stayed with him.

Our Dad built for him in the backyard a rabbit hutch, on extended legs, with occupant, so that Brian could see from his bed. In so doing, the arrangement ultimately resulted in establishing in me a permanent antipathy towards cats. I heard Brian cry out in distress from his bed. 'Jim, there's a big cat trying to get my rabbit.' It was a very large, tiger-striped, local tom, tearing at the netting of the hutch door. Quickly into the kitchen, I quietly opened the door and sprinted towards the feline interloper.

On hearing the sounds of my approach, the cat panicked, choosing the wrong direction of escape. My recently developed rugby football talent helped the animal over the backyard gate.

Brian was my brother; someone had to take care of his rabbit, so why not me? Eventually he was up and about again but was left with residual cardiac weakness of subsequent significance. The semi-feral cat permanently steered clear of our rabbit.

Our home of 2 Elm Street fitted our needs admirably. It provided all seven of us with room for personal needs. While we lived there, my Dad significantly improved the property, both inside and out. He was a competent early devotee to DIY. He also made sure that his children made appropriate contributions.

In my case I particularly and ruefully recall assisting my Dad in the repapering of the sitting room. The ceiling, twelve feet high, demanded rudimentary scaffolding for Dad and me. My help proved painful occasionally for Dad, as my juvenile attention wandered.

The yard-broom I was using to support the paper that Dad was, before me, pasting to the ceiling, slipped and gave him a painful blow behind his ear. Somehow, I managed to repeat the dose again. Exasperated admonition, while massaging the injury, came: 'Jim, pay attention! Watch what you're doing!' But I was not dismissed from the job!

The staircase was about six-foot wide, wood-panelled, and with substantial mahogany balustrade. This area was where I learned about sandpaper grades, rubbing-down, and rudimentary efforts at applying varnish. At the time, it was not very interesting; I would much rather have been outdoors. But my Dad's tuition gave me a thorough grounding in caring for property that served me well throughout my life. And duly, the lessons were passed on to my children.

Regrettably, our life at 2 Elm Street was shortly to come to an end. We seven were to move into property in the adjacent Varley Street, and the vacated Elm Street was to be taken over by Granddad's surviving younger sister, Great-Aunt Edith Alice.

There was a single, solitary, advantage to leaving Elm Street. This concerned the electrical power supply. At the top of Elm Street there stood one of the many town cotton-mills. Normally powered by a steam-driven engine, mill equipment was routinely operated through a system of overhead drive shafts, pulleys and continuous leather belts.

For some reason, the mill atop Elm Street had some machinery that was electrically powered. And, extraordinarily, the power supply was Direct Current (DC), distinct from the almost universal Alternating Current (AC) in the rest of Colne. The irritating result was that the whole of Elm Street was compelled to use the same, DC, power. For lighting, radios, and radiant fires, DC power was acceptable. But for any electric motor-driven equipment, like our vacuum-cleaner and Scales washing machine, only DC motors could be fitted.

It was an extraordinary arrangement, the manufacturer abusing his position to dictate to the surrounding populace. Both my Granddad and my Dad heaved a sigh of relief as DC electricity was left behind.

As, indeed, was the Scales washing machine and the vacuum cleaner, to be replaced by uniformly standard AC-powered equipment at our new home.

Yet another move

The change of occupancy of 2 Elm Street took place in the summer of 1939. Great-Aunt Edith was the wealthy member of my Granddad's family. She had been the principal beneficiary of Great-Granddad's estate.

For a woman of her considerable assets, it seemed odd that she remained unmarried into her fifties. She was to be cruelly betrayed in marriage.

The prospect of her, and her intended, together occupying the spacious property at 2 Elm Street was probably appealing to them. But the man involved, at the kindest, could be described as an opportunist, a scheming adventurer, a charlatan with an eye for an opportunity. Long after the above situation, with me now a married man, my Granddad, unusually, expressed himself graphically about the union. In fact, there was no union. To use Granddad's description, 'He were battin' fur t' other side.'

Sadly, the advice he tried to give his besotted sister was ignored. Great-Aunt Edith went ahead with her foredoomed marriage. On her early death, the husband promptly disappeared, taking with him the significant residue of Great-Aunt Edith's wealth. Thankfully, the Elm Street house legally reverted to Granddad.

Soon, events in Europe began to have local impact. School summer holidays were reduced to two weeks, in a concerted effort to free railways for more urgent traffic.

For the balance of our holidays we were required to report to the school at the normal starting time. Teachers were allocated groups of pupils for whom organised activities of a localised nature were arranged. The recently opened outdoor swimming pool at Marsden Park in neighbouring Nelson was a popular attraction. The summer of 1939 was particularly hot. The handicrafts teacher, a dedicated dry-fly trout angler, was deputed to oversee a fishing trip to the canal. Poor man, he had no conception of our crude coarse-fishing methods, with float and a worm for bait. Our chemistry teacher, Mr Robinson, father of my Park School friend Peter, conducted a party across the nearby moors, to the Corn Close Bore hole, where emerged our local, spring-supplied town water.

That water, bubbling out of the ground, and prior to treatment by the Water Board, was unbelievably wholesome and palatable. The chemically loaded product we are now supplied with is an absolute travesty relative to that at the Corn Close Bore. I have never forgotten the taste of that genuine, fresh, untreated cold water.

The associated treatment plant demonstrated practical chemistry. Much more of interest was the nearby Laneshaw reservoir, clearly alive with trout. Regrettably, it was too well protected for any attempted personal incursion.

A bike ride took us to nearby Lothersdale, to me, a very familiar location. Some of the party did not appreciate the long, steep climb to en-route Black Lane Ends. The free-wheeling helter-skelter down the following descent was a bonus for me, but not for all.

Few of my classmates shared my passion for the outdoors; they failed to understand, for example, the significance of the heated lime kilns, still then in operation at tiny Lothersdale The Parish records there listed the names of local men who followed their Squire and Henry V to the field at Agincourt. History. The site of the nearby Pinhaw Beacon I never failed to visit. In past times of national concern, a beacon-bonfire was lit. It was an early warning system, transmitting information before mobile phones. And at that location, in the winter of 1804/05, while waiting for signs of signal bonfires to the south, in warning of the threatened Napoleonic invasion, the local beacon-guard, Robert Wilson, was frozen to death at his lonely post.

J.W. Foulds

I always, then, and still when possible, thank that tenacious and loyal man before I leave the area. Sadly, not many of my classmates felt so keenly about our local history.

But the most significant event of that period, which I still recall with indignation, was a mass cycle ride to Malham, about eighteen miles distant. This was one of Dad's more familiar destinations, either alone or with family. Gordale Scar, Malham Cove, and the Tarn were all favourite locations.

On my way to school on the appointed morning, my rear wheel suffered a puncture. Quite competent to deal with the problem, I soon carried on to school, puncture repaired.

The cycling party had left without me. It was no problem for me to follow the route; I knew it well. I duly arrived in Malham half an hour behind the main group. My sense of satisfaction was soon severely deflated by a sarcastic and public humiliation from the headmaster. He was contemptuous of my failure to arrive at school for the scheduled departure and simply refused to hear my explanation. The man was a bully.

Not too long afterwards the headmaster was able again to demonstrate his superiority over the author. I had committed the unpardonable sin of chewing gum in class.

Sent to the head by the maths teacher, I received three very painful strokes of the cane. The pain was not only physical; I was outraged at the abuse of adult authority. We were never physically punished at home.

A day or two later, I was donning my pyjamas before bed, when my Dad spotted my bruised buttocks. He was outraged; after questioning me, he instructed me to dress again. My feet barely touched the ground as we made a bee-line for the head's home in nearby Keighley Road. Leaving me outside, Dad battered on the door until the head appeared. The two disappeared into the house, so I was not a party to the subsequent conversation. The head was left in no doubt about any possible repetition of my thrashing.

I would like to be able to say that never again was the head able to cane me. Disgracefully, I was subsequently caught acting outside of the law once more—smoking a cigarette in the boys' lavatories.

I think the totally unsympathetic head knew that I would not let Dad know about this particular misdemeanour. He certainly applied correction without mercy.

Meanwhile, we happily settled in Varley Street. Additional to the usual 'two up and two down' room arrangement of local terraced housing, there was also a generous working kitchen and a substantial attic bedroom. Grandma and Granddad used the front bedroom still with their wedding, furniture, in sumptuous, but age-darkened elm wood. In the back bedroom were my sisters. Additionally, there was in that room, a porcelain wash-basin and bath. In the flagged yard there was a coal shed and 'tippler' toilet.

The large attic bedroom housed a double and a single bed for Dad, Brian, and me. The first to retire took choice of beds; after that, it was Hobson's choice. The only heat was that radiated from the flue wall, by the living-room fire smoke en route to the chimney pot on the slated roof top. Conditions in the attic bedroom in Winter-cold. But we were hardened to the conditions and sleep was never a problem. In deep winter, we occasionally had the luxury of a 'Valor' paraffin oil stove. During winter, the normally tilting, roof-light window was invariably frozen shut. Central heating? What's that?

Although less generous than Elm Street, we really had no space problem. For Brian and me, externally, there was additional opportunity for expansion. The cobbled, back, Varley Street was unusual. On the one side were the houses, and facing was an area of hen-pens and gardens.

But more importantly, there was a footpath on both sides of the street. We were able to play our street cricket on both pavements.

As a left-hand batsman, I had the freedom of the 'pitch' on one side of the street, while the others—Brian, the Wilson brothers, Arnold Woodcock, and the Irving brothers—all batting right-handed, used the opposite pavement. A small but vital facility, I could execute my favourite hook shot over the houses. 'Six and out!' Of course, we were restricted in our back-street games by mothers. At that time, the street could be totally barred by successive rows of laundry pegged on lines across the street. Mondays, traditionally, were a particularly bad day: 'Washing Day'. The delivery of coal or milk by cart also presented continuing battles. Cricket? On Monday? No chance!

Together with the various gardens and hen-pens in our locality, there was also an active homing pigeon community. We were fascinated by the constant overhead exercising of these birds as we worked in the garden. Our Dad, ever practical, was more interested in the clearance of waste from the lofts for use as manure for our crops. For a brief spell, I joined in the practical operation of a nearby loft. Apart from 'mucking out', I also, weekly, took in their basket the birds selected for that weekend's race. At the local Pigeon Club HQ, the birds were fitted with a unique rubber ring on one leg. The details from each ring were duly recorded and the loft's own timing clock set, sealed, and returned to home lofts to await the return of the birds.

Additional to the breeding, rearing, and training of the birds, there was also a busy social activity centred on the club. A man's sport.

During the racing season birds were progressively trained to fly increasing distances, culminating in cross-channel races from France or even Spain.

Complementary to the local Club prizes, generated from entry fees, there was also a significant gambling content. And possibly even more importantly, successful birds, or their progeny, could change hands for significant sums. None of this concerned me; the personal thrill and excitement came on Saturdays, sitting at the loft awaiting the return of our birds. From an elevated location, the owner, Mr Hatfield, watched keenly down the expected return route, along North Valley Road. He had developed extraordinary bird-recognition capability. He could identify pigeons from a distance of several hundred yards, all the while giving out a running commentary. 'That's one for Barnes,'—a competitor

'Yon two's away up Trawden.'

And then at last, 'Here's one of ours.'

On one memorable occasion, in a race from Nantes in France, he had spotted a cock bird we had entered. But he then said, 'He's bringing a stranger with him.' When, eventually, both birds had alighted, the rubber race ring removed and inserted in the timing clock, he was able to examine the stranger. It was a hen bird who, by her obvious behaviour, had been attracted to our cock bird. Extraordinarily, her home loft was in Belgium. She turned out to be a jewel. With the cock bird she had chosen to follow, she produced a succession of profitable progeny. Apparently, even in the world of pigeons, hormones are powerful.

After each race, the recording time-clock was quickly taken to the Pigeon Club. There each clock was opened to ensure that the rings from the returned birds matched the time recorded. Eventually all the day's returns would be listed; a simple formula of actual distance travelled to the home loft, divided by the flight time taken, identified the winner in yards/minute. The flying speed of these birds was unbelievably high. Dependent on weather, an average speed for a race in the UK of 40 to 50 mph was not at all unusual.
The only release point I can now recall is Mangotsfield near Bristol, a distance of almost 300 miles. Birds released at 9 a.m. would arrive at our loft at about 3 p.m. And for a race from the continent, it would be at least double the distance. It's an admirable bird, the homing pigeon. There could, of course, be disasters. Totally weather-dependent, a returning flock meeting adverse conditions could be literally decimated. An added hazard was raptors like peregrine falcons. The loss of birds not always accepted with resignation.

How did they find their way home? It is still apparently a mystery. For me, there was absolutely nothing like seeing our pigeons returning to the loft following a race. The hair literally stood up on the back of my head at the sight of a returning bird. And, still, a puzzlement.

I cannot recall why my association with this sport ceased. Perhaps it was World War II, when pigeons served a more important national utilitarian role. While my involvement lasted, it was riveting. The time I spent in the world of the homing pigeon was enthralling, exciting, even mysterious. Now, almost seventy-five years later, I still on Saturdays can see pigeons speeding overhead, en-route to their more northerly lofts. And, briefly, I am young again.

War

The catastrophe facing the world as Adolf Hitler demanded '*Lebensraum*' for the German people at the expense of other European nations, was not allowed to have too severe an effect on us children. We suspected, generally, that 'something' was developing, but we were shielded from the reality. On the Sunday morning of 3 September 1939, Brian and I were, as usual, up at dawn, and with fishing tackle heading for Lake Burwains.

In the nearby tower of the Foulridge parish church of St Michael's and All Angels there was a pleasing bell carillon that rang sweetly across the lake. On Sunday mornings, it played familiar hymn tunes, using high-pitched, possibly silver, bells—not the deep, resonating, repetitive 'rounds' of the heavy bronze bells of Colne Parish Church.

The particular Sunday was a beautiful, sunny, warm, and still September morning. The bells rang out across the water, calling the faithful to prayer. I was not to know that I would never again hear them. Thereafter, they were silenced for the duration of the war—except on government instruction, such as to warn of imminent invasion, or, more cheerfully, to announce a welcome victory for our forces in far-off lands. And, further, my life was soon to change significantly, taking me on paths away from Lake Burwains.

On that Sunday morning we had no inkling that the world about us was changing forever. I heard some men, fishing nearby, talking quietly together, and on hearing one say, 'The balloon's really gone up,' I searched the skies, but found no balloon. Later, at home, we began to notice changes around us. Life was, simply, never the same for us again. There were heavy curtains across the windows for something called 'blackout'. The few, but increasing, motor vehicles were all fitted hoods with p narrow slits across their headlights. In preparation for potential siege, a wooden box of various foods was packed away under the staircase. For the first time in our lives, we heard the wailing note of the air-raid siren. Suddenly, many other things began to change. The street lighting disappeared. Adults, going out after dark, carried hand-torches; their use, however, was sparing, as the supply of batteries became difficult.

Familiar fruits from overseas were, at best, scarce; more commonly, they were simply not available. Food rationing was soon introduced; typically for a week there was four ounces of butter, eight ounces of bacon, and twelve ounces of sugar. In a milling economy, white flour and bread totally disappeared, to be replaced by a form of wholemeal containing mysterious flecks of a darker grain.

We youngsters were unaware of the catering struggles faced by our Grandma. The earlier experiences during the Depression years prepared working-class women for the increasingly hard times ahead. Their young, characteristically, were sheltered as far as practicable from harsh reality. Air-raid shelters rapidly appeared; 'ours' was built on land below the junction of North Valley Road and Skipton Road. For a time, following the sirens sounding, Dad would gather all us children and usher us into that cold, damp, unlit place. Thankfully, as time and events dictated, we abandoned the protection of the shelter.

At school, our principle games master disappeared into the Armed Forces, to be replaced by a lady gymnast. Other restrictions relaxed;

it was no longer a requirement that a blazer be worn. The manufacture of such 'luxury' items was suspended in deference to war production. A school cap with badge was all that was required.

Colne and Nelson Rugby Club closed down for the duration of the war. There was an established close connection between the school and that club. Star players in the school's first fifteen were quickly introduced into Colne and Nelson teams. One of the principal characters at the town club was Dr J.D. Robertson, a general practitioner from Barnoldswick. It was no surprise when he joined the staff at the school on an ad-hoc basis. It was apparently not a universally welcomed arrangement, however. There is no doubt in my mind that Doc Rob, as he was generally known, performed a sterling service in keeping rugby alive at the school throughout the war years. We were able to maintain matches against some other schools. Closely neighbouring establishments, accessible by public transport, were the normal opposition.

The winter of 1939/40 was bitter, the coldest for years. For me, the paper round with the *Daily Worker* was a painful affair of frozen and chapped hands, coupled with bruised limbs whenever my bike slipped on icy cobbles. The skies at night, clear, frosty, and bright, were reflective of a total absence of pollution from street lighting. For the first time in my life, the ethereal, shimmering, glowing majesty of the aurora borealis spread directly overhead. The night skies were resplendent with a myriad of twinkling stars, the Milky Way spreading across the whole sweep of the skies. It was a quite different appearance from the nights we now witness.

Despite the total use of coal for fuel, with the resultant plumes of perpetual smoke, the night skies were visible to a degree unimaginable today. Whether for economy or not, I can no longer recall, but breakfast porridge was cooked on a paraffin-fuelled Primus stove. We all quickly became adept at firing up this device. The first to rise in the morning soon had the equipment hissing away. Somehow we youngsters were never able to disguise the taint of paraffin in the porridge. Later, we all joined the Youth Hostel Association. The Primus stove was standard cooking equipment in many of the hostels, with limited, fundamental, cooking facilities. No problem to us.

At school, I had found several kindred, birds' nesting, spirits. One such lad had ventured even further than egg-collecting; he had fostered an abandoned, fledgling magpie, which he successfully reared on a diet of worms, slugs, caterpillars, and puppy biscuits soaked in Oxo liquor. From time to time, Everard—for that was indeed his name—brought the bird to school concealed in a stout carrier bag. With teachers unaware, it sat in the bag by the side of Everard's desk. The occasional squawk was quickly silenced by the rapid transfer of a soggy dog biscuit.

Another active egg-collector was Barry Sunter. His father, Joe, was the editor of the local newspaper. He was a spirited protagonist of my Dad's repetitive, political, 'Letter to the Editor'. Barry and I, extraordinarily, cycled about 100 miles to collect a black-headed gull's egg from the nearest gullery, at Ravenglass, in West Cumberland. This must surely have been an exhausting, painful, even perilous journey, of which I have absolutely no recollection. My mind must have eliminated the suffering.

Later Barry was to join his father's journalist profession. He ultimately achieved national eminence with one of the then Manchester-based broadsheet newspapers. As my contribution to preparation for the national war-footing, I joined the local, 431, squadron of the Air Training Corps. Soon, I had my first ever flight, from the nearest airfield, at Salmesbury. The twenty-minute experience, both thrilling and frightening, was in the rear, open seat of a Tiger Moth biplane. By comparison to that first nervous flight, subsequent commercial flying, on scheduled airlines, was a distinctly boring affair.

As the wonderful warm summer of 1940 extended into an Indian autumn, the Battle of Britain was being fought out in the skies over southern England. We had one such brief incursion, in, I think, October of that year. A number of us from school were at the tennis courts of the local, Alkincoates Park.

Suddenly, totally without warning, there roared overhead the black shape of a German aircraft. It was no more than 100 feet above us, and I was able, briefly, to see the helmets of the crew in the nose and the German insignia on wings and tail.

My recent ATC tuition in aircraft recognition confirmed it as a Heinkel 111. Apparently, a few minutes earlier, this aircraft had dropped some bombs on the village of Chatburn, only a dozen or so miles distant, on the opposite side of Pendle Hill. There had been fatalities; we later heard that this intruder, based in Norway, had been destroyed by RAF fighters. It was a brief glimpse of the potential horrors of war—an interruption to a gentle game of tennis in a relative backwater.

The town's schools began to take in increasing numbers of pupils from towns remote from Colne Evacuees, and their impact, demands separate treatment. Some events are not exactly in chronological order; it is not significant to the account.

Evacuees

The respected, late, author and playwright, Jack Rosenthal, produced in 1975 a television play *The Evacuees*. It featured the experiences of two young Jewish evacuee boys in World War II Lancashire. The events portrayed were, in fact, autobiographical; Rosenthal and his brother were evacuated from Manchester.

Although it was not contemporarily, he and I shared attendance at two Colne schools. I was always uncomfortable with some of Rosenthal's recorded experiences in that play. He and his brother were, the play recorded, treated less than sympathetically. In my experience, their reception contrasted unfavourably with other, similar, events personally observed. I felt that true Lancashire hospitality was traduced by the play.

In 1936, arising from the civil war in Spain, my Dad and a number of his Communist associates were responsible for the arrival in Colne of a party of refugee children, mostly from the Basque region. One young boy, Luis Sanchez, was the same age as my brother. They attended the Park Schools together; later, they were apprentice butchers together. It was a friendship that lasted seventy years, only ending in 2006 when Brian died. Luis was to follow, three years later. Luis's surrogate, warm, welcoming, and loving family, Linda and Malachi MacDermott, happily adopted their Spanish evacuee as their own son. Ultimately, he was their sole beneficiary.

In 1938, two foreign girls joined my grammar school class: Marianne Mouhren and Lydia Heldenbusch, contemporaries of the celebrated, doomed diarist Anne Frank. These two girls had been spirited away from Germany, thereby escaping the unbelievable future fate of so many victims of murderous Nazi tyranny. I do not recall any reaction to these girls other than a warm and sympathetic welcome—despite national and ideological differences.

Soon after the outbreak of World War II, the St Bede's Grammar School, from Bradford, was briefly evacuated to Colne. They happily integrated with their Lancashire hosts. Although they stayed only briefly in Colne, friendships flourished. As a Catholic school, their pupils—like some of their Colne classmates—did not join in Protestant-based school prayers each morning. Otherwise, integration seemed totally harmonious and welcoming. Following the December 1940 blitz of Manchester, the North Manchester Boys' High School was evacuated, and integrated into Colne Grammar School. Similar to the St Bede's pupils, some of the North Manchester students followed differing religious faiths. Apart from the obvious exclusion from morning prayers, all quickly integrated into the host school routines. Many made significant, sporting contributions. As could reasonably be expected of a Manchester school, their winter game was association football. But they rapidly adapted to the rugby code played at Colne Grammar School. So much so that significant numbers played for the various Colne, school teams, and with no little success. The more mature members of the single-sex

Manchester school gleefully integrated into the mixed-sex Colne school. *Girls*! Friendships formed and developed.

Independently of official evacuations, following the bombing of Merseyside, families arrived in Colne seeking safety. One such family, the Waters, included son John. He attended Colne Grammar School and joined my circle of friends. Freed from urban restrictions, he enthusiastically embraced the outdoor activities of our childhood. Our free-spirited wanderings were occasionally a distress to his parents, unaccustomed to offspring not returning home before nightfall, as was normal for us Foulds children.

For his part, John was soon part of 'our gang'. He was one of the band of brothers dedicated to the stocking of the pond in the disused Castle Road quarry. Possessed, inevitably, of the characteristic Scouse accent, John was a very welcome evacuee, and he certainly integrated more happily than was apparently the lot of the Rosenthals.

My Great-Aunt Cissie welcomed one of the Manchester High School boys. As the dangers in Manchester apparently receded, the official 'residency' of their school at Colne came to an end. Before he returned to his Manchester home, Great-Aunt Cissie's guest gave me his sports cycle. It replaced my own, recently stolen, bike. It provided for my transport needs for a further fifteen years. It was another demonstration of mutually agreeable integration.

On this question of the welcome typically afforded to evacuees to East Lancashire, we again refer to the sterling efforts of Great-Aunt Hannah and husband Fred. Their Grandchildren remain in warm contact with evacuees of sixty-five years past cared for by Hannah and Fred. Although still saddened by the recorded experiences of Jack Rosenthal, in his otherwise entertaining play, I am simultaneously reassured by my own experience of true Lancashire, the warm hospitality, in the integration of strangers.

The welcome greetings and the hospitable treatment of such a disparate collection of unhappy young people counters that apparently experienced by Rosenthal. The treatment offered him was quite uncharacteristic.

There is now, sadly, another side to this, usually welcoming characteristic of Lancastrians. The arrival in our county since World War II of so many others has no doubt demonstrated that we all have our limitations. Sometimes we can all be pushed beyond our elastic limits, and difficulties arise. The East Lancashire warmth of my childhood is now less evident.

Early war events

Gradually, as 1939 ended, wartime restrictions began to impact domestically. Inevitably there was increased concentration on food production, as imports decreased under increasing activity of German submarines.

The passenger liner *Athenia*, carrying British children to safety in America, was torpedoed in the Atlantic. Another submarine penetrated the Royal Navy anchorage of Scapa Flow, there sinking at anchor the ageing battleship *Royal Oak*. In both cases, there was heavy loss of young lives. Good tidings were almost non-existent. But, for Christmas 1940, there was at least one cheering event in an otherwise bleak panorama. The Royal Navy trapped the marauding, successful, German surface-raiding, battle-cruiser *Graf Spee*, in the River Plate estuary, off Montevideo. Rather than face battle, the German captain Lamsdorff scuttled the ship and took his own life.

On mainland Europe, there was, apparently, stalemate. During the bitter 1939/40 winter, the German settled for non-aggression. The defending allies were similarly quiet.

During the year, our Dad had enrolled Sylvia, Brian, and me into the Youth Hostels Association. Further, he had acquired a tandem cycle. Resulting from his attack of rheumatic fever, Brian's heart had been weakened. For him, cycle trips temporarily meant him occupying the rear seat of the tandem. Dad, Sylvia, or I would take the front seat, supplying the major pedal power.

It became a pleasant weekend diversion on the bikes to head for the nearest youth hostel, Jerusalem Farm, at Black Lane Ends. In the grounds of this hostel, at a height of about 1000 feet, there was a stark reminder of the recent past, potentially perilous childish ailments like scarlet fever or diphtheria. There stood an abandoned, rudimentary isolation hospital building. It had corrugated cladding and, no doubt, equally austere internal furnishings. Thankfully, none of us children had been compelled to suffer such isolated incarceration in this remote building, one only recently relegated to history.

The wardens at Jerusalem Farm Hostel were a startling pair. They were Robert Gummerson and his wife Dorky, she a pure Romany. Their family consisted of an extraordinary Labrador dog, Punch.

He was a very skilful and entertaining performer of tricks, patiently taught to him by Robert. The dog could carry out simple arithmetic and could growl an audible and comprehensible response to Robert's enquiry, 'Punch, are you hungry?' It was a repertoire that kept the audience highly amused.

At the time, the dog became well renowned for public, charity performances in the north, even appearing on radio. Sadly, television was not yet available. Following a performance for hostellers, Punch would circulate with the appropriate charity box, collecting coppers. The dog habitually ensured that some would be extracted as his reward, to be used to finance his 'goody-bag'.

Photograph 19 shows Punch performing one of his tricks—playing dominoes against a hosteller. He seldom lost.

Warden Robert was a locally recognised eccentric. Even in winter, he wore open sandals, without socks. He was also typically adorned in a tattered jacket, a pair of corduroy trousers held up with farmers' bailer-twine—frequently lacking a shirt or vest, all topped off by a beret. He was a determined and heavy smoker; it was normally a Peterson pipe, with a bowl large enough to take a half-ounce of tobacco. But behind this diverting appearance, he was a highly intelligent, informed, well-read, and widely travelled individual.

His wife, Dorky, equally striking, had long, flowing, shining, black tresses and deep-set dark eyes, clearly suggestive of Romany ancestry in furthest Eastern Europe.

Probably the catalyst for my Dad's strong and enduring friendship was political. Both the Gummersons were active party members. Dad's visits were clearly not solely associated with his love for the outdoors. Their friendship and mutual interest continued into the 1950s at a succession of hostels opened in Wharfedale, with the Gummersons the initial wardens. My Dad in later years acted as an unpaid, honorary warden.

About this time, I was introduced into a fringe political group, the Left Book Club. With our family being passionate bibliophiles then, the Colne Carnegie Public Library was a regular destination. Now this passion extends to my Granddaughter. Genes are extraordinarily powerful things.

The Left Book Club, studying the offerings of publisher Victor Gollancz, met in the Shackleton Hall in Nelson. Forming a discussion group, the topic of each meeting was that particular month's offering, at a cost of half a crown per copy (12.5p). Books discussed were those like Orwell's *The Road to Wigan Pier*, Robert Tressel's *The Ragged Trousered Philanthropists*, and Dr Hewlett Johnson's *The Socialist Sixth of the World*. Johnson was the dean of Canterbury Cathedral. Clearly an ecclesiastical dissident, he was an embarrassment to the Establishment.

My involvement with this group did not prosper. The subject matter discussed failed to excite my interest. Possibly it was too demanding. In any case, the study of books was redolent of reluctant school commitment.

Additional to the Left Book Club offerings, my Dad also subscribed to other, worthy, magazines like *The Psychologist* and *The Dalesman*. This latter publication was then produced in the Dales' village of Clapham, where author and playwright Alan Bennett now retreats to his parents' retirement cottage. Then, it was the locality of one of our favourite cycling destinations. And if memory serves me correctly, my Dad was also a spasmodic contributor to the magazine. "Dalesman"

My progress at the grammar school was less notable than it should have been. Although I was blessed with the required intellect, few of my teachers could be described as inspirational. As the end-of-term reports stated: 'He could do better.' Meanwhile, my Manchester trips continued. In the skies above the city, the barrage balloon defences floated. As events unfolded, they were to be found wanting.

In the spring of 1940, in the lowlands of Holland, Belgium, and France, the war erupted. The German blitzkrieg attack was unleashed, irresistibly driving the defenders backwards. The British army retreated to Dunkirk, and evacuation to England.

About this time, at the top of Skipton Road in Colne, I was astonished to meet Dad's friend Saul Clitheroe. He it was who had given me my first 'big' bike.

I was unaware that he was a member of the Territorial Army. And there he was, in a dishevelled army uniform, unshaven, carrying his kitbag on his shoulder, but without rifle.

Saul had been evacuated from Dunkirk, and he was on the last stage of return to his home to rest. He was very pleased to see a familiar, friendly face, possibly blotting out some of his recent experiences. He opened his kitbag; inside it was brimming with cigarettes, 'liberated' from abandoned NAAFI stores in France. He and I had often shared fishing at Lake Burwains, so he was aware of my addiction. We parted, me clutching a twenty-packet of Players, Saul heading for a sleep in his own bed. Providentially, he was to survive the war.

Somehow, the perilous nature of our country's situation did not, even then, dawn on me. I lacked imagination, apparently in more than a single sense.

As 1940 closed, my sister Sylvia increasingly tried to involve me in feminine plans. Girls are more alert to pubertal changes than boys. Sylvia had noted that her elder brother was undergoing change. I was quite unaware; I hadn't even noticed that my voice was of deeper register. Sylvia tried, without success, to direct me towards her interested girlfriends. I failed to respond, at least for a while. As a boy with two sisters, and accustomed to co-educational schools, the presence of girls was accepted as normal. But clearly, change was afoot. The march of time could only be briefly delayed.

Dad was now working at a Trawden cotton-mill, Forest Shed, operated by the Pickles family. We children continued to visit him occasionally. Under the pressure of war, work was plentiful in the textile trade. However, established working practices in cotton-mills were undergoing radical changes. As in World War I, when the young men were called into the Armed Forces progressively their tasks were taken on by girls and young women.

In the preparatory area where Dad worked, two of the men had already been called up. In their places were a young, married woman and, more significantly, a slim, attractive, and shy girl. The latter's name was Mona Weir. She was of my age group; she had, earlier, aged fourteen, started work as a reacher-in for Dad.

Soon, she was being trained into the higher skill of chain-beaming. In this operation, bales of coiled cotton were progressively separated into individual threads, and meticulously wound, as warp-threads, onto loom-beams in designated colour and pattern sequence, prior to the weaving function.

It was a demanding and skilled operation, previously exclusively reserved for men. There was, normally, a premium training period when the operative literally paid to be taught the skill. Now, here was this wisp of a young girl competently operating this complex machinery, very few weeks from initiation, on a level of pay in excess of that earned by a weaver. The fact that I actually noticed her was indicative of my hormonal changes. I was not to know it then, but that shy, engaging, competent young girl would become my wife. Then, there were no exploding stars or bells ringing. But later . . .

Soon, hormones really did begin to play havoc with my system. A succession of septic spots, boils, and carbuncles literally erupted all over my body. Briefly, I was a walking pustule.

'Go and see Dr MacAuley,' instructed my Dad. When I entered his surgery, Dr Mac's face brightened. 'You're just the lad I wanted to see!' he exclaimed. 'I've got this stuff we need to test for the Forces, and you're the ideal test-case.' The use of my body in an experiment did not seem unreasonable, in the circumstances. Duly, Dr Mac gave me a single injection, and he instructed me to return after seven days. Magically, all my eruptions disappeared; septicaemia was vanquished. I have never, since that action, suffered any form of pimple, spot, or boil. And the injection? Penicillin.

My experience is exemplary proof of the effect, nearly seventy years ago, of Dr Fleming's antibiotic, medical, revolution. The changes I experienced were quite astonishing. What is without doubt is that, from that day, I have been totally immune from any form of septicaemia. How desperately sad it is that the subsequent inappropriate use of antibiotics has effectively eliminated the powerful antiseptic capabilities that I was fortunate to benefit from almost seventy years ago.

In a possibly less dramatic sense, there was earlier in Colne a very significant social benefactor. This memoir would be incomplete if it lacked some reference.

The nationally recognised Hartley's jams have original Colne roots. William Pickles Hartley and wife Christina in their time significantly and gratefully recalled their origins with a series of magnificent, generous, public-spirited social initiatives. For the townspeople of

Colne, they donated the then, magnificent modern Hartley Hospital, built between Colne and Laneshaw Bridge. It was a stunning, stone-built structure, with generous windows overlooking to the south the Pennine hills and moorland. For the sick, it provided a bright, open, aspect. I made there, in 1942, my solitary visit, to donate the first of a continuing succession of blood-donations.

Conveniently adjacent to the hospital, the Hartleys also financed the building of the Hartley Alms Houses for the elderly of the town. For the young mothers, the Hartleys financed the building, in Barrowford Road, of the Christina Hartley Maternity Home.

Sadly now, as a result of the relentless centralisation policies of the NHS, there is no longer a hospital or a maternity home to carry the generous name of the Hartleys in Colne. Only the Alms Houses remain to record the debt of gratitude owed to them. Sir W.P. Hartley lies buried in Trawden Cemetery.

Coincidental with my hormonal activity, but almost certainly unconnected, my scholastic performance improved. I appeared to produce results more equivalent to my potential. Or, possibly, my improvements arose because of my more inspiring tutors.

Whatever the reason, the improvement resulted in my topping the class and being awarded a prize. I chose *A Bird Book for the Pocket*, written by, I believe, James Fisher.

Characteristically, no-one at home made any particular fuss. They were probably relieved that I was, ultimately, making an effort to match my potential. The financial burden I represented was never mentioned; there was not even a hint.

The war situation continued with the Germans in the ascendancy. Despite the heroism displayed by the RAF in the Battle of Britain, it sadly served only as a brief breathing space.

The assault by the German air force was switched to night-time. Following the initial targets of London and the South, as 1940 closed, cities like Coventry, Birmingham, were also bombed. On the night of 22/23 December Manchester was attacked by 270 aircraft, and 272 tons of bombs were dropped.

Although we were familiar with the sounds of enemy aircraft overhead, thankfully we were not to suffer any bombing. On only a single occasion did we actually hear the sound of exploding bombs. It happened about the time of the Manchester blitz. A single German aircraft returning to its base in Norway jettisoned two bombs that fell on the lower slopes of Tum Hill. There were no casualties; but my Dad's cousin Donald was visiting us that night. When the bombs detonated, he was visibly shaken, and he remained disturbed for some time. He it was who had endured the Coventry blitz. He was unable to forget the trauma; as the Tum Hill bombs exploded he was immediately transported back to Coventry. A few weeks following the Manchester blitz, when transport was operating more normally, Dad sent me to the city on a routine trip. Much clearance had been achieved, but the sight of so much damage was a shocking revelation.

A change of school location

Following the 1941 summer break, we at Colne Grammar School returned to education in a brand-new, architect-designed, modern building. It was a rural location, along Barrowford Road, surrounded by playing fields. It was an establishment where study would be undisturbed by the usual sounds in the urban position of Albert Road.

It included all the latest in specialised room designs, modern laboratories, art studio, and a dedicated gymnasium. Importantly, it also had excellent dining facilities. In comparison to Albert Road, it was a revelation. Although currently no longer used as an educational establishment, this splendid building now has appropriate protected status.

Resultant on war-time restrictions and labour availability much of the external landscaping was incomplete. For a considerable spell allocated games periods instead diverted pupils into unskilled labour aimed at correcting external errors and omissions.

A single rugby pitch and a girl's hockey pitch, which in summer would be used for cricket, had been completed. These areas, denied specialist ground staff attention, were overgrown with pervasive weeds like docks and dandelions. Parties of pupils, particularly during the lunch-time break, dug out such plants, by the roots. Great piles were stacked across the playing areas, awaiting disposal. I do not recall too much dissension; the effort was, surely, in our own interest.

The second rugby pitch, situated at the rear of the school, was traversed by an existing generous, field-drainage ditch. For an extended period, the whole school, at designated games periods, was instead dedicated to completely filling this ditch, and creating a level playing field.

There was, of course, no mechanical aid; all work was completely manual. I remember a broken door being pressed into use; loaded with tree-stumps, branches, fence posts, boulders from the adjacent stream bed all tipped into that wretched ditch. The work was done repetitively, until, weeks later, the top was levelled with stream-gravel and a final skim of soil. Of course, as the land fill settled, there was a continual topping-up. We did, ultimately, play games on that pitch. Somehow, the ground was never water-logged! The drainage was excellent, unlike the principal pitch. There, the drainage was dreadful. From the damp days of autumn until early spring there was standing water somewhere on that field. Under our continuous use, a morass of stinking mud was generated. When I returned home with filthy kit, I was barred entry into the house until everything was immersed in a bucket of water in the backyard to be, subsequently, hand-washed by me.

My Grandma was never to wash such equipment. Dad insisted that I learn to care for my own gear. I was married before a loving wife relieved me of that chore And, even then, I had to be careful not to upset the laundress. If I spoke out of turn, I would find that my rugby shorts had been crisply starched. A spirited lass, my dearly beloved. I digress.

The physical effort needed to level the second pitch was no problem for me; I had been working in our garden for years. Thankfully, the work on that field eventually ended; manual, unpaid labour was acceptable on family terms. It was certainly not a substitute for rugby.

As a contribution to the national 'Dig for Victory' campaign, an area of almost two acres of the playing fields was converted into vegetable production. The labour force was predominantly supplied by the juniors. I resisted on the basis that I made an independent contribution in our own garden. Hormones had begun to strengthen my will.

The increased travelling distance to school meant that it was no longer possible to return home for my midday meal. The new school facilities, of course, included splendidly equipped kitchen and dining areas. Contrary to modern dissatisfaction at school meals, I have nothing but praise for those provided for us at the grammar school. Our cook, Mrs Barritt, and her team were magnificent. At a cost of 6d each day, the food was excellent value. Freshly cooked on the premises, under war-time limitations, it was almost miraculous.

Local, special buses transported us between home and school. The Burnley, Colne, and Nelson transport organisation provided travel at extremely attractive terms. A pack of ten tickets was sufficient for a week's travel at a cost of 3d. Extraordinary value.

For me, the most significant change continued to be the, apparently, improved quality of the tuition. Some of the teachers at Albert Road had retired, and, of course, we were all ourselves maturing and developing more adult appreciation. It certainly seemed that teachers were increasingly able to inspire more interest in their subjects.

W.G. Kellaway took the higher level of maths tuition. 'Taffy' Thomas was the senior French tutor. He was a typically dark-haired, short, wiry, and passionate Welshman. Both of these dedicated men, also with the assistance of Dr Robertson, took care of school rugby.

'Taffy' loved to get directly involved in practice games. Some of us also seized the opportunity to rough-up a teacher. He was quite well aware that he could take care of himself. Was there ever a Welsh rugby player who could not? 'Taffy' had very poor eye sight, and the more devious of us on the playing field would take the opportunity to have a joke at his expense. We knew from past experience that if the ball was in the air, Taffy lost his bearings. He would quite often follow a passing crow, waiting for it to behave like the ball and return to earth. It was a schoolboy joke that we managed to inflict on Taffy at least once a game. He was a very popular member of staff, and he earned our respect.

T.H. Land taught senior English. He was an excellent tutor. Jack Rosenthal described him as 'inspirational'. Chemistry continued to be taught by M.R. Robinson, known disrespectfully to us as 'Micky'. Previously, he had fought in the trenches in World War I. We soon learnt that we could craftily divert chemistry lectures from the established curriculum into, instead, him describing the practical application of the subject in the manufacture of explosives. With Mr Robinson duly galvanised, the whole chemistry period could disappear in a lecture on the realities of trench warfare, under German shrapnel bombardment. In retrospect, I suspect he knew what we were doing, and like any competent teacher was able to engage our attention, at the same time imparting the required syllabus in a more interesting manner.

All of the above teachers were, in my experience, excellent. My attention in class improved, as my later achievements were to demonstrate. Sadly, our arts teacher, Mr Watts, was totally unable to instil in my Philistine soul anything remotely artistic. When, subsequently, examinations arrived, as predicted by Mr Watts, art was the sole subject at which I failed.

An important feature of war-time life concerned the constant surveillance and protection of major buildings. Under government direction, all had to be provided with an over-night fire-watching service. Dad was required, from time to time, to present himself for such duty at the market hall.

Inevitably, there were times when his more urgent, political, activities took precedence. When such clashes arose, I would be deputed to attend in his stead. I enjoyed it, particularly as I was paid the magnificent sum of half a crown (12.5p) for the ten-hour shift. It was exploitation, clearly leading to the ultimate legal adoption of a minimum wage!

At the school, the same basic principles operated. The nightly fire-watch teams were composed of a master and two senior male pupils.

We were now well accustomed to the wailing sound of the air-raid siren, as German aircraft droned overhead, en-route to industrial Lancashire, Merseyside, Northern Ireland, and Scotland.

Thankfully, we were spared the trauma of attempting to extinguish a fizzing magnesium incendiary, using only buckets of sand and of water, and the stirrup-pump provided. Somehow, it did not seem to be adequate precaution. As night fell, it was possible, from the school roof, to see the sinking sun glinting on the Manchester balloon barrage. It was a reminder that we were fortunate that our locality was rurally scattered and unlikely to suffer the fate of urban areas like Manchester or Liverpool.

On one of my scheduled fire-watch nights, I noted that the master in charge was the maths teacher earlier responsible for my initial caning by the head. I still carried a sense of suppressed outrage that the particular maths teacher had created. I knew well the sixth former who was also on duty that night. During the time preceding our night duty, he sought me out and advised me that our master was confidently rumoured to undertake nocturnal activities not associated with fire-watch.

He had been told, confidentially, that the master actually left the post during the night. A lady was, allegedly, involved.

If events emerged as rumoured, the sixth former had a plan to deal with the situation. He would take responsibility for any outcome. I thoroughly approved of his proposals. I still felt, deeply, the sense of injustice at the pain that that master had caused me. I welcomed any opportunity to redress the imbalance. In the event, following a shared supper, the master wished us a good night and retired to his separate quarters. After an appropriate delay, the sixth former went to ask the master a minor question. His room was empty; it was time to activate the 'plan'.

All outer doors were doubly locked; keyholes were stuffed with paper. The headmaster was phoned and told of the situation. We then retired.

At about 4 a.m. we heard efforts to enter the building, which we ignored. Before morning classes, we were interviewed by the head. The master dared not approach us; he knew he'd been rumbled, although we were not told the outcome. That teacher was not a popular man; I had never forgiven him his part in my flogging four years earlier for the childish misdemeanour of chewing gum in class.

Revenge is a dish best eaten cold. My dish was all the sweeter for its four-year maturing. Peevish, I know.

The road ahead forks

Although I had begun to produce improving work and results at school, I was adamantly determined to leave at the first possible opportunity. Wiser heads at home counselled continuing education. I was stubbornly and stupidly determined to enter the labour market at the first opportunity. Maths/Rugby master Kellaway also had suggested that the wiser course for me would be to stay at school.

Quite probably, Dad had appealed for his support. It was to no avail; soon after the forthcoming school certificate examinations it would be my sixteenth birthday, and I could then put schooling behind me forever.

Winter turned to spring; revision for the school certificate examinations began. Summer arrived, gloriously hot. Brian and I spent much time at Lake Burwains meeting our final bait-supply commitments to the Burnley miners, particularly our friend Jimmy Topping. Soon, we would be 'old friends'.

Brian spent time fishing; I lounged at the water's edge, revising *Eothen*, *The Coming and Passing of Arthur*, and *Richard II*. School certificate examinations were more demanding than their successors, the GCSE. It was for our generation a requirement that a candidate was required to pass a minimum of five subjects at the one time to achieve the School Certificate. Anything below that number meant failure and a year's additional study before a resit. It was something that concentrated the mind wonderfully.

The first of my examination subjects was art. Although no Michelangelo, I surprised myself by actually enjoying the test. In the event, it was a false dawn. Mr Watt's assessment of my abilities proved to be accurate. I duly failed that examination.

I do not recall much concerning other subjects except for the French oral examination. Taffy Thomas had prepared us well; I genuinely enjoyed the dialogue in a foreign language held with a complete stranger. Twenty-five years later, working in industry, Taffy's tuition proved its worth. I was the sole foreign language speaker in an engineering department, meeting a posse of a dozen foreign visitors all confessing only a smattering of English. Taffy did us proud!

Summer holidays arrived. With the Air Training Corps I spent a week in a furnace of a Nissen hut at the RAF Station on Walney Island near Barrow. This camp functioned as an air-gunnery training base. Some of us were actually allowed to seat ourselves in an aircraft turret and blast live ammunition from four machine guns at

A Lancashire Past

a distant 100 yards' target placed before sand-filled butts. Noisy, but exhilarating, the implication was lost on immature minds.

The more unfortunate cadets were taken on a thirty-minute' terrifying flight in one of the resident Harvard aeroplanes. It was a very noisy and nauseating craft for the innards of the uninitiated cadets. The pilots seemed to sadistically enjoy inflicting on their passengers a hair-raising trip along the Lancashire coastline, hedge-hopping over the three piers of nearby Blackpool. It was very frightening.

The realities of war-time food rationing were brought graphically to our callow notice at meal times, where we were served the same food as the RAF ground staff, quite unlike our home-cooking. Breakfasts were bread and margarine. Lunch was greasy gristle and undercooked vegetables. The mugs of 'tea' had remote associations with Assam, or Darjeeling, and they were heavily dosed with bromide, intended to suppress male sexual urges. Local fish and chips were in big demand off camp.

Home, and soon the examination results were published. There was none of the histrionics currently prevalent at the equivalent times. In my case, I simply opened the *Manchester Guardian* and looked for the Colne results. I cannot recall any of us actually attending school to precisely identify results gained.

I made my ultimate 'postal' visit to Manchester. A further six years would pass before I returned to that city. Brian should have been with me, entering the labour force, as a fourteen year old. In his case, Dr MacAuley counselled caution, based on his weaker heart. It was sound thinking, which was ultimately greatly to Brian's advantage. His entry into the workforce was delayed by about six months.

Mid-August, I returned to school for my final foreshortened term. Placed in the 'scientific' lower sixth form I was expected to briefly study pure maths, applied maths, physics, and chemistry. The only significant impact originated from Mr Kellaway. Intended as an early introduction to the lofty heights of calculus, we were all allocated the task of writing a 1000-word essay on our personal choice of three eminent mathematicians from a list of twenty.

It was designed to provide early exposure to the disciplines of self-study and research in the school library. Those students with the expectations of higher education would benefit. In my case, it provided a continuing opportunity for Kellaway to sit by my side in the library and continue insidious family pressure for a change of heart. Stupidly, stubbornly, I resisted; I would not listen to logic.

The project we had been set proved vastly interesting to me. Ignoring the obvious 'names' in the proffered list, I elected to write about Riemann, Lobachewski, and Gauss.

In the case of the latter genius, I can still clearly recall his classic 'Law of Natural Distribution'. An absolutely basic premise concerning the natural allocation of talent, intelligence, size of cranium, size of fruits, and so forth, which is so utterly immutable, was predicted by this German mathematician and is still not understood by many.

The fundamental natural premise is that all are not equal. Some are more, or less, equal than others. The task is to accept this reality and organise events and actions within the prevailing limits. In my later sad experience, it is a law not accepted, or possibly not understood, by the Trade Union movement.

My essay must have impressed Kellaway. Nearly seventy years later I can recall quite clearly the comments he made and the mark allocated: twenty-nine of a possible thirty.

Presenting me my work, he made one last, unavailing attempt to change my decision to leave school. In arguing his case, he instanced the essay I had written as proof of the course my life should be following.

In the final few weeks at school, I had, independently, sought employment of interest. There was no official assistance, then; careers advisers at school had not yet become a valued support.

There was, of course, no difficulty in finding a job. The task was to seek out the most appropriate opportunity. After two or three interviews that failed to excite my interest, I was called for interview at the Rover Company's war-time works at Sough Bridge near Earby. The post I sought was in the works chemical laboratory.

My appointment was scheduled for 2 p.m. When I presented myself, I was informed that the post had already been filled. At 10 a.m. a school friend and fellow member of the rugby teams, Fred Heap, had pipped me to that post. The circumstances were to influence the rest of both our lives. The Sough Bridge Works personnel department re-directed me for interview at the sister factory at Bankfield Shed, Barnoldswick. The post on offer was in the inspection department of the jet engine test beds. The prospect appealed, and I accepted the job.

I was a foolish, headstrong boy; I swapped my life of a five-day week, of six and a half hours a day, for that of a wage slave. The working week was fifty-eight hours, Monday-Friday, 7.30 a.m. to 6.30 p.m., and also Saturday, 7.30 a.m. to 4.30 p.m., with one hour lunch break each day.

For this toil, I was to be rewarded at a rate of one pound, five shillings and three pence (£1.26). National Insurance claimed one shilling and ten pence (9p). The balance of £1.17 was for my Grandma to feed and clothe me—theoretically. In fact, she received very little. My daily travel and food costs swallowed twelve shillings (60p). For my personal weekly spending, 37.5p, leaving roughly 20p as my net contribution to the family Exchequer.

I duly said goodbye to very few of the staff at the school. On 16 September 1942, I departed Colne Grammar School for the final time as a pupil. My Dad and my Grandparents were unhappy at my action. But I was always encouraged to seek my own salvation. My choice of career had, equally, been left in my hands. My sixteenth birthday was significant for only one reason; it was the first time in my life to that date that I could actually recall the date being of any significance. Previously, birthdays simply came and passed by, ignored. I literally cannot remember a single occasion when a birthday was celebrated with a party. Not in our family, nor in the lives of any of our contemporaries.

This was, quite simply, symptomatic of the times. Money was too limited for such superficial activities as a party. The one significant birthday was the one when schooldays were left behind, forever.

Duly, on Monday 21 September 1942, at 6.55 a.m., I waited with others for the special buses that transported workers to Barnoldswick from the districts of Burnley, Nelson, and Colne. It was the end of my life as a boy; a welcome new day in the adult world dawned. A broadening and exciting horizon beckoned.

About the Author

Working-class Lancashire; born 1926 in a cotton textile town.

Original family was of flexible character, possessed sporting abilities, and held free-thinking social values, passed down to descendants.

A childhood of rural wanderings in Lancashire/Yorkshire borders.

A scholarship grammar school education was abandoned at age sixteen to join the World War II workforce.

Engineering apprenticeship, on the, then, secret and revolutionary Whittle jet engine.

Higher education continued by day-release and extended night classes.

Married at twenty-one to talented local dancer spasmodically attached to London blitz escapees, Sadlers Wells Ballet Company. A marriage lasting sixty-two years.

Together shared thirty-five years life of developing progress at successive RR factories to senior management level.

A family of one daughter and one son.

Left RR for directorships at the UK base of a Swiss company of precision machine tool manufacturers. Simultaneously an evening, senior visiting lecturer in management subjects at a nearby college of further education.

Disillusioned departure from industry, to share with wife the purchase and eleven-year operation of a small, private hotel in Cumbria.

Sold the hotel and for seven years jointly operated a business of antiques and collectables. Associated wide caravanning tours of the continent seeking stock for the home business.

Despite two years of devoted parental home-nursing of daughter, lost to leukaemia. Wife, devastated, lapsed into Alzheimer's. For five years, nursed at home by author. Widowed 2008. Cathartically wrote this story.

Son and daughter-in-law, both graduates, with one daughter. An accomplished dancer, including ballet, she is following in the footsteps of her Grandma.

About the Book

This book concerns a vanished world.

From 1926 birth, the year of the General Strike in the UK, the life of, and significant influences on, a working-class boy.

Industrial Lancashire location bordering the Yorkshire Dales. Family struggles in the cotton industry and a World War I diversion.

Active participation in Trade Unionism and local Labour party by Father and Grandfather. Father, ex officio.

Three siblings, all soon initiated into the connection between work and money, coupled with the necessity for food production from hens, allotments and the countryside.

Parental marriage breakdown. Rescue by loving, extraordinary Grandparents. Overcrowding and a nomadic lifestyle.

Father, increasingly politically active. Secretary of local branch of Communist party. Author, soon a trusted messenger. Surreptitiously collecting correspondence 'officially' considered seditious and earlier feared intercepted by 1930s' Special Branch.

Family habitually and totally committed to the open air and associated rural pursuits. Rambling, cycling YHA. And at a time long before total motorised domination and ecological concerns.

Blessed with an above-average brain, selected at ten years for grammar school education, in a pioneering wave of local working-class children thus 'privileged'.

An educational system and atmosphere unprepared for and unwelcoming to the children of artisans. Enthusiastic sporting commitment, mirroring the wider family involvement.

A stubborn adolescent, determined to resist family wishes and pressure to follow higher education, joining the war-time labour force aged sixteen.